KATRINA SOUL SEARCH

Finding ourselves amidst the post-hurricane chaos

By

Ben Messner
Martin Schoffstall
& Seth Barnes

Published in Gainesville, Georgia, by Praxis Press, Inc.

Editorial assistance provided by RobertSutherland.com

Book design by LarrySmith.com

Cover photo by Getty Images/Photodisc

Praxis Press, Inc.
3630 Thompson Bridge Rd. #15-100
Gainesville, GA 30506
www.praxispublishing.com

Printed in USA

ISBN 978-0-9754305-2-1
ISBN 0-9754305-2-1

Some of the names in this text have been changed to preserve the identities of the people involved.

To Order Additional Copies of *Katrina Soul Search* go to www.PraxisPublishing.com

ACKNOWLEDGEMENTS

The person who put more actual time into this book than anyone else was Robert Sutherland. He helped us churn out draft after draft with deadlines looming. Robert is a great copy editor. Check him out at www.RobertSutherland.com.

We would like to thank Alli Mellon, Janeen Messner, and Talia Barnes. They not only lived the stories in this book, but wrote about them. "Soul Search" wouldn't have happened without them.

The First Year Missionaries themselves were wonderful examples of Jesus with skin on. They are ministering around the world to "the least of these" as this goes to press.

Marty would like to thank Diane, Derek, and Evan, "Who I could not have done this without, and the people at Schoffstall Associates who did their jobs and also mine while I was gone."

TABLE OF CONTENTS

Introduction...1

August 28, 2005
    Some Memories...4

August 29, 2005
    Janeen's Journal..6

August 30, 2005
    First AIM Team..7

August 31, 2005
    A Day of Prayer...9

September 1, 2005
    A New Day...12

September 2, 2005
    Life Can Change..14

September 3, 2005
    Salvation Army Center...18

September 4, 2005
    Baton Rouge...21

September 5, 2005
    Update..24

September 6, 2005
    Ben's Prayer..26

September 7, 2005
    The River Center...29

September 8, 2005
    Our First Miracle...*32*

September 9, 2005
    In the Shelters..*40*

September 10, 2005
    Alli's Story...*53*

September 11, 2005
    Bright Lights 24/7...*71*

September 12, 2005
    Final Day..*79*

September 13, 2005
    Call for Reinforcements......................................*90*

September 14, 2005
    A Challenge to Consider......................................*94*

KATRINA Soul Search

KATRINA SOUL SEARCH

Finding ourselves amidst the post-hurricane chaos

INTRODUCTION

By Seth Barnes, Executive Director of Adventures In Missions

As I write this, it's been three weeks since Katrina. I've been to New Orleans twice and am doing OK. By that I mean, the city's throbbing pain hasn't overwhelmed me. A thirteen-year-old named Tony, whose house is in shambles, brought it near when his voice broke describing how he felt. As did Alice Adams, an older woman with no carpentry skills. She begged for help – she reached out through me and begged the Church for help. The mold on her home's walls was creeping higher. Her wet rugs needed to be torn out.

For a moment, Alice and Tony took on the face of New Orleans and came near my heart. Their pain went beyond the CNN reports and became three-dimensional. In responding, I moved from the posture of a passive observer, almost a voyeur, and became three-dimensional.

Yesterday I hopped a plane out of that city that is really just an oozing open sore, and within hours was in the sane oasis of my home. Last night while watching Monday Night football, my friend ventured a comment that touched the rawness of the place where Tony and Alice live in my memory.

"We can't all respond to this thing. We can't have a bunch of cowboys running around."

"That's hardly the problem," I said, "So few people have responded personally. If you sent me 500 cowboys tomorrow, I'd give them all drywall knives, divide them into ten groups, go to ten neighborhoods, and cut away wet drywall."

"But it's my impression that the Church has responded pretty well," he persisted.

"Relative to what? The need is overwhelming. How many Alice's are there tonight asking God for help? The Church is responding institutionally, but it's up to each of us to respond personally."

Specifically: after the drywall and carpet, there are roof repairs, and after securing homes, people need to walk a path that will fill them with love and hope again. And beyond that, fragmented and bitter communities need to be stitched together. The question of how you resurrect and sustain hope hasn't begun to be answered.

Surprised at the edge in my voice as I spoke to my friend, I apologized to him for my passion and resumed watching football.

The danger of the calamity that is New Orleans is that we will collectively and permanently do what I did last night – return to our regularly scheduled programs. The danger is that it will go the way of the Tsunami or whatever the "disaster de jour" was before that.

New Orleans is different. It's not just another FEMA project. A city twice the size of Nagasaki in 1945 has been devastated. An American city.

While the mainstream media has lost the plot, debating the nuance of words like "evacuee," and passing the political blame for breached levees and bungled evacuations, the Church is in danger of missing its greatest moment since the Civil Rights movement.

Remember, Martin Luther King was a pastor. His marchers were congregation members. Their cause required an activist response by the body of Christ.

Justice and mercy exist at either extreme of the same continuum. The balance between them can only be maintained through an activist posture. But whereas the Civil Rights movement required the activism of a just cause, Katrina requires the activism of a merciful heart.

These kinds of compelling opportunities only come along for the Church once in a generation. This is our moment. It will take at least three years to put many of New Orleans' families back on their feet. We can't switch the channels. We can't look away from the Tonys and Alices. To do so would be to surrender the one great chance that we, as the body of Christ, may have in our lives to reaffirm our corporate identity as healers and difference-makers. It would be to turn our backs on our destinies.

By the time you read this, the drywall on most homes might be pared away. The roofs might be covered. But New Orleans' pain will still be raw and the opportunities to touch it will be undiminished.

Adventures in Missions (AIM) exists to connect the Church to ministry. Like everyone, we had the opportunity to consider, "What is God asking us to do in response to Katrina?" Just as we still have that opportunity every new day we wake up.

This is the story of how AIM answered that question.

August 28, 2005

Some memories are indelible. Meeting that "special someone." A call from a hospital emergency room in the middle of the night. Billy Graham's voice at a Crusade saying, "Come. Come now. The buses will wait." Smoke venting from the World Trade Center Towers. Hurricane Katrina.

We've heard enough of wind velocities, barometric pressure, paths, projections, and seen enough weather reporters standing in the rain. There is good news though! God is alive. He cares. He is bringing healing to the people who have been hurt so deeply. And He is using regular, average, normal people who have dedicated their lives to Him to do the job.

Life for millions would be normal again if this were merely a nightmare from which they could awake, rub their eyes, have a cup of strong coffee and go back into autopilot for the rest of their days. But, this nightmare was and is real. For some it might never end. All we can do is care and give aid, and offer to bring Christ into their lives.

This book is all about what happens when soldiers of Christ become His caregivers.

The Executive Team of Adventures in Missions (AIM) met on Wednesday, August 31st to seek God's guidance on how He wanted AIM to be involved in the Hurricane Katrina relief efforts. The watery floods in New Orleans and the subsequent human floods at places like the Superdome could not be ignored — even though "that's not our department." The pictures of families stranded on rooftops, pleading for water and the basic essentials for life were overwhelming.

Our response began with AIM staff member, Ben Messner.

<u>Ben Messner:</u>
I am sitting in a hotel room in North Carolina on the final day of a men's retreat. The past few days have been full of paintball, honest

sharing, steaks grilled over open fires and new friendships formed. The guys in the room with me are ahead of their time for sure when it comes to Kingdom accomplishment.

I am exhausted. I realize now that Janeen and I never really recovered from the last eighteen months in Africa. I could fall asleep and not wake up for days. At the same time, I feel my heart once again breaking for a needy people. For the last few hours, the TV has mapped out the possibility of the complete destruction of New Orleans. Hurricane Katrina is the name of the storm barreling toward over one million people.

The guys seem a bit casual about this situation. My heart is pounding. I know we need to pray. I call the guys together and we kneel by our beds and cry out to God for the salvation of the people in the path of Katrina. I know the Lord has already broken my heart for this deal.

My prayer is, "Lord, show me how to respond to this, as you desire."

From Janeen Messner's Journal:

I was sitting at a cozy coffee shop in Chattanooga enjoying spending time with my friend, Aimee. After a while, I called my husband, Ben, who was doing a retreat with some guys. They had planned on camping out overnight, but decided to go to a hotel instead because of expected rainfall caused by Hurricane Katrina.

I only spoke with Ben briefly, but I remember he mentioned how bad the hurricane could be and how he had been praying hard for God to divert its path away from where it could do a lot of damage. I had not seen or heard much news that weekend, so I didn't think much more about it.

August 29, 2005

<u>Janeen's Journal:</u>

I drove back to Gainesville. About an hour into the trip, I hit a lot of rain and thought of Hurricane Katrina. I got home and met up with Ben. No one said much about the hurricane, so I figured that it must not have been as bad as people were thinking. We went out to dinner with some friends and prepared to get up early the next morning. We were scheduled to help provide leadership for a training camp for 13 students who were leaving soon for the mission field.

<u>Ben Messner:</u>

The retreat ended and we all took our wives out for dinner tonight. A random Asian food place was chosen and we piled into cars to go there. The rain that hammered us along the way was crazy. Tornadoes ripped through a nearby county destroying 30 homes. The effects of Katrina are felt all the way out here.

August 30, 2005

THE FIRST AIM TEAM RESPONDS

Ben accepted responsibility for a team scheduled to spend the next three months in various countries with AIM. He'll lead them to Atlanta for a three-day mission trip at a homeless shelter called "Blood n Fire" (B&F) before they go overseas.

By now, the levies had broken in New Orleans. The destruction was beyond imagination. Relief was needed badly and quickly. We, at AIM, considered sending a First Year Missions (AIM intern) team to New Orleans to serve.

We got flashbacks to the calamity and intensity that followed 9/11. There was nothing we could do in 2001. This time will be different. We knew God was calling us all to action.

We had given our word to minister at B&F. We needed to check with our contact there, Bill Britton, and make sure that we had a blessing to be released from our ministry there. Just in case. When we called, he said that we needed to make a decision within the next hour, so that he could make other arrangements.

We started making calls to people we knew in Louisiana and Mississippi. We called a few organizations that were helping with relief efforts, but we had no success with any of them. They either were not answering calls or said they had nothing arranged or organized. A couple of places took our name and number, but never returned our calls. After 45 minutes, we had made no progress; so, we met together again to pray.

There were many feelings and impressions that people had. The unifying call, however, was that we were to go to Atlanta and help at B&F. We knew we must stay open to the leading of the Holy Spirit. We knew that God could give us opportunities to help, even if it wasn't right away.

The team went to B&F and arrived around 4 pm. After settling in and having a quick meeting/tour, they served dinner in the shelter and began building relationships with the people there. They met that evening and talked about possibilities for the following day.

Bill Britton said he was going to try to reach someone at the Salvation Army to see if we'd be able to help somehow with "Katrina" the next afternoon.

August 31, 2005

This turned out to be a day of prayer. We didn't gather together to tell God what we were going to do — we sought His will.

There was prayer in the Executive Team meeting. Afterward, it was clear that the Lord wanted us to submit AIM's resources to the "first responders" to this tragedy.

Samaritan's Purse began to refer people in need of housing to us. Calls began coming in. One of our staff members organized a database to match those who had room to spare with those who had nowhere to go. We could not keep up with the calls. Yet, even more had to be done.

Back in Atlanta, as we prayed and asked God for direction in the morning we believed we were to go to the Salvation Army center in Atlanta, but we still did not have the green light to go. So we carried on with our planned activity for the morning.

EVACUEES ARRIVE IN ATLANTA

We served breakfast at B&F. At around 9 a.m., we met together to go out into the city to practice "listening prayer" – that's when we try to be quiet before the Lord and listen to what is so often called His "still, quiet voice."

We all went in different directions in small teams. The idea was that we would listen to what God might be saying, whether it was to hang out with the folks who were traveling with us, to engage in conversation, or to quietly pray for whatever we felt God was asking us to bring before Him.

Eventually one group went to a park and met a man whose entire family lived in the Lower Ninth Ward of New Orleans. He was very worried about his family, especially his grandmother. They lived in one-story, small homes and he had not heard from any of them since Katrina had hit. He was holding a newspaper and staring at images of the damage. One of the photos was of his street immersed in deep water. He lost his wife last year to cancer and said that he was at peace with what "Allah willed."

We knew evacuees were coming to Atlanta because we met some of them on MARTA. One family said that they lost everything in the hurricane. They all piled in their car with their pets and ended up in Atlanta. They also said that they were expecting 20 more relatives to arrive. They all were trying to fit into one apartment because their landlord was charging them so much.

A GOD STORY

When we got back together, we prayed again and this time we felt like were to go to the Salvation Army. Bill told us that the Salvation Army (SA) headquarters was not far away. We liked the idea about going and decided to pray to see what God would say as we traveled there. We wanted His will more than our own. As we drove we still believed He was leading us there, so we went and showed up at the door, ready to help.

Bill and Ben went into the office to see what we could do. When they came out they said that we were going to drive to a different location because that was where help was needed most. The crazy thing was that the people inside the office already had the directions printed out in case a volunteer team showed up to help. They were that desperate.

OUR FIRST TASTE OF CHAOS

We arrived just as the evacuees started to pour into the area. Walking through the doors there, anyone could have felt the tension inside. The front room was filled with people who needed assistance because of Katrina. We later discovered that the police had arrived a few minutes before we got there to calm a man down. Evidently, he was upset because SA workers could not give him more and better food.

The SA staff was not ready for those first few overwhelming days of evacuees arriving, although they were working extremely hard and doing all they could. Joy was the person we met. She connected us with the people who would direct us.

We were taken to the gymnasium where tables had been set up, all scattered and spread out. Then the SA leaders showed everyone the donated goods and asked us to make some sense of it all. We broke open box after box and put vegetables on one table, fruits on another, meats on another, beans and soups on another. Then there were the wonderful random donations of things that seemed to have no category. Corn and green beans overtook the place.

The rhythm of our system was broken after a couple hours of focused work. We heard the news that gas was running out and that it might be out for days. Prices were jumping to $3 or $4 a gallon, so our drivers took a break to fill up the vehicles. The Salvation Army asked us to return, if possible, the next day. We went back for three more days.

In debriefing that evening, we all felt the weight of Katrina in a much more tangible way. This was the first day we had met evacuees and seen the devastation and shock in their faces. We knew that the scope and effect of the storm was enormous and would take more work to heal than we could imagine.

September 1, 2005

A NEW DAY

We woke up energized and overwhelmed, looking forward to being able to help again at the Salvation Army (SA). It was as if living and eating in a homeless shelter was preparing us to better be able to serve the evacuees we met during the day. It gave us a taste of what it is like to have nothing.

After serving and eating breakfast at B&F, we went to the SA center that now had a big sign out front reading, "Hurricane Disaster Relief." Many more boxes were waiting to be doled out. Donations flooded in all day long. So did evacuees. Things were dragging along, however, because SA only had four staff caseworkers. They were nice, but they were just so outnumbered.

The waiting area was extended into the gym, where we were sorting donations. We had evacuees surrounding us as we worked. They waited and waited and some grew very irritated. Others were just tired and hungry. But nobody was able to grasp the enormity of what had just happened.

Sorrow was in the air we breathed. We felt it fall on us several times that day. We would glance over and see someone trying to fill out a form. It was no longer rational to ask for typical personal information such as address, profession or phone number. In fact, it was crazy. There was an artist who had just lost his entire studio, all his plans, work, tools, computer and home. How was he supposed to fill in the blanks? His whole life was now a blank that couldn't possibly be filled in.

People were being told it might be months before they could return home. But nobody even knew if they had a home left <u>standing</u>.

We paused a few times while sorting goods and went over to talk with people, to listen to the journey that brought them here and to share the weight of their pain. We prayed with a family who had a baby born two weeks prior to Katrina. The baby was actually due the day Katrina hit but, as the grandma said, "He knew he had to get out early."

Something sparked in us today — it made us aware of our desire to be more involved in helping in this crisis. We processed that feeling much of the day.

BROKEN HEARTS

As our group drew together that night to pray we sensed that we gathered with broken hearts. We saw people of nearly every social class affected today. "We lost everything; we have nothing left to go back to." These horrible phrases pound us and are driven deep into our souls. But this is not "about us." We're the lucky ones. We haven't lost anything. Just the opposite. We have gained new insights into the suffering of man. And into Jesus Christ — who volunteered for action to save mankind.

Ben's Journal:

The Church is slow to respond thus far. It's as if the reality of this has not hit yet.

What will make that change? Talk won't change anything. We pray that God will use AIM to effectively serve the needy and to mobilize the church to respond.

This is a long-term disaster. Today, it was about manning the call center, sorting donations, counseling evacuees and praying. Next week, it will be about getting people settled into homes. The month after that it will be something different. Next year...

We are ready to go back tomorrow. No, not just ready. Excited to be used by the Shepherd to feed and love His sheep.

September 2, 2005

LIFE CAN CHANGE SO MUCH IN A WEEK.

Janeen's Journal:

After packing up our things, we left Blood and Fire. Ben and I knew that the next few days might be days of organizing and preparing for further involvement. Our drive was packed with friendly silence. We only spoke in scattered thoughts.

On Thursday of the next week, we were responsible for coordinating a "boot camp" for young adults (18-24) at AIM's headquarters in Gainesville. Ben began mentioning the idea of moving the upcoming training camp to Baton Rouge. I thought it would be great idea; perfect training grounds for intense ministry situations.

Everything at the Salvation Army (SA) seemed to be running so much better. There were many more volunteers. Large-scale systems were in place to manage all the donations. Evacuees were arriving in greater numbers. The SA folks really knew what they were doing now. Volunteers were still needed to be caseworkers and to do organizational tasks. We told the SA staff we'd come in early the next day.

A SURPRISE E-MAIL FOR THE MESSNERS

Ben Messner

Janeen and I finished with the AIM intern team this morning. At lunch, my phone kept ringing the whole time. The most random call was from Mark Almand, a recent acquaintance from the AIM network. He asked if Janeen and I were going to say "yes."

My response was, "Yes to what, Mark?" When he realized that I did not know what he was talking about, he read an e-mail sent to me from Seth.

AIM was going to respond to the Katrina crisis in a big way, and I was the suggested leader of this response. I was freaked out by the opportunity and yet I wanted it at the same time. I told Mark I needed time to pray with Janeen.

A SURREAL MOMENT

By the time Ben and Janeen walked into the AIM office that afternoon, the word had spread that AIM was responding to the crisis and that they were the likely leaders. It was a surreal moment, almost like in the movies. Ben later reflected that it felt as if people peered out at them as they walked down the hallway to Seth's office so they could talk and pray together about how to respond.

AIM had sprung into action. Seth sent this memo less than a week after our busy, happy and meaningful annual staff retreat in Dahlonega, GA...

Since we left the retreat center, Hurricane Katrina has laid waste to the lives of hundreds of thousands. Because we exist to mobilize and equip the Church for missions and because we've done a lot of mission work in New Orleans, it was only natural for our leadership to consider how God would have us respond. We prayed about it and God told us to mobilize the Church for this particular mission. In the last two years, God used us to respond to the AIDS crisis in Swaziland and to the Tsunami; times of great human suffering cry out for the ministry of Jesus' people.

I took a call from a person who also felt God wanted him to help. He was a pastor who had buses waiting to head to Baton Rouge after the service on Sunday. Lots of people have that same desire to help.

In Baton Rouge, a city whose population has swelled by 150,000 in a few days, our good friends have been relaying

stories of all the broken people showing up with nothing but their despair. The needs in each place are as compelling as they are endless.

The word continues to spread. Nathan Clay just sent out an e-mail to the 25,000 people on our mailing list. Mark Lindberg designed a database to connect those needing housing with those offering their homes. Ben and Janeen are praying about doing the AIM intern training camp in Baton Rouge. Here in Gainesville, we have set up a "war room" with charts on it seeking to bring order out of the chaos.

America has never experienced a natural disaster of these proportions. The Church must rally. We at AIM must rally. Jesus will show Himself strong through many of you in the months to come. Many people have come to us and said, "How can I help?" We're organizing as quickly as we know how. We need people to cover the phones. We need volunteers to do legwork in places like Baton Rouge and Houston. And, of course, we need prayer. Please contact us, if the Lord prompts you to help.

Yours for the Kingdom,

Seth

PREPARING FOR BATON ROUGE

Ben and Janeen had to decide quickly if we should relocate the First Year Missionary (AIM intern) training camp to Baton Rouge, as a relief team. In just a few days, 50 college-aged students preparing for 90-day trips to the uttermost parts of the earth for Christ would arrive at AIM Georgia for pre-field training. What would happen if we went to Baton Rouge? God seemed to be leading us there.

Janeen and Ben sat down with Seth in his office and informed him that they were ready to respond. They were tired but willing to lead the AIM intern teams out to Baton Rouge. As the decision to relocate the camp spread through the office, the response was immediate.

We still did not know what to do about bringing all 70 people involved in the AIM intern training camp to Baton Rouge. It seemed crazy since all the preparation to that point revolved around thinking that the location would be Gainesville. Alli Mellon, the AIM staff member in charge of the trips, called. She was "with us" if the plans changed. Typical of her, but a relief anyway.

Another thing we had working in our favor was a church, River Community Church, that was welcoming us to come, stay on their property and minister out of there. A good friend of AIM's, Steve Wallace, serves at the church and was helping us make connections.

Janeen's Journal:
Again, we spent time asking God what we should do. This was the first night we felt very led to go to Baton Rouge.

Late that night the notification went out to the AIM intern's by email: "Prepare for Baton Rouge, rather than Gainesville."

September 3, 2005

BACK TO THE SALVATION ARMY CENTER

We went back to the Salvation Army center today with more workers. The place was overrun with evacuees and volunteers. The line of cars driving up to donate supplies was backed up all the way to the road. Finally, people had responded!

Later, Ben sent a letter out to mobilize resources, funds, and volunteers...

> *Greetings!*
>
> *"Have you ever felt like you were created for such opportunities that currently face you?"*
>
> *The answer to that question for Janeen and I right now is a definite "YES!"*
>
> *The crisis of HIV/AIDS and its related issues of poverty, hunger, and orphans that we faced in Swaziland, broke us down in every possible way. Yet, we found our hearts to be fully alive and our relationship with each other and the Lord to be growing stronger than ever. Then, the Lord flipped things upside down again and called us back to the United States.*
>
> *Soon after we arrived home, the director of Next Step Ministries at AIM decided to move his family to Swaziland. Seth asked us to take over the position until December. We accepted the call, loaded up a car that we borrowed from Janeen's parents and moved to Georgia to work out of the home office. Then disaster, in the form of Hurricane Katrina, devastated our country.*
>
> *This past week, Janeen and I served meals in a homeless shelter. In the afternoons, we found a ministry that has now changed our life in yet another direction. We*

served at the Salvation Army command center that is caring for the evacuees flooding into Atlanta from New Orleans.

Our hearts were broken and we looked for AIM to get involved. That's exactly what happened. Starting next Thursday, Janeen and I are leading a team of 70 into Baton Rouge to serve the relief effort there. There is a key AIM contact who is in a great place to serve thousands of the more than 100,000 evacuees that have flooded into Baton Rouge. We will come under his leadership and establish AIM in that area as a "qualified relief organization" for both the immediate crisis and the long-term need.

Our team will minister in several ways:
• praying with and counseling evacuees and service workers
• aiding distribution efforts
• conducting children's programs in evacuee shelters
• connecting other organized relief efforts.

We will be a self-sustaining army of volunteers. We'll do anything and everything the Lord opens for us to do. A primary goal is to mobilize the church and to establish opportunities for evacuees to move into the homes of host families.

If you're wondering what you can do, please consider donating funds through AIM. Your money will quickly make a direct impact on the refugees. Also, consider serving through AIM. Over the next several months, we will be conducting multiple trips into devastated areas and you could be part of such a trip.

As we face this grim situation, Janeen and I once again feel our hearts rising up and coming alive. We *believe we were made for an opportunity just like this. Though the trip is only scheduled to last a few days, we do not know how long we'll be there. We are simply answering the call! Our heart is crying out for the church to arise and fulfill her destiny.*

Please join us in this effort through your funds, your time, your supplies and most definitely your deepest prayers. Thank you for continuing with us in this journey.

Chosen to Serve,

Ben & Janeen

September 4, 2005

BATON ROUGE IS OUR PLACE

Baton Rouge emerged as our first staging area. We were beginning to hear reports from our friends there. As of last night, 148 families had signed up to host evacuees. We have people on the ground working hard to find families who are ready to go. We relayed this message from Michael Paul, a friend living in Baton Rouge.

> *Seth,*
>
> *Sorry I have taken so long getting back to you. We have been swamped taking care of the 17 people living at my house.*
>
> *I have not yet been in the large centers. I will get Red Cross training and clearance to go into the centers beginning tomorrow.*
>
> *A friend has been in all of the centers here and suggested, as far as the people who want to host these families, that they should come here and walk through the centers, meet the people and let God provide divine appointments.*
>
> *Some host families have already had bad experiences. Hosting strangers is a huge responsibility for families and churches. There are risks. Housing and food are the least of the needs outside Louisiana. Schooling, jobs, health issues, financial support, etc., will all have to be worked out.*
>
> *Hosts need to understand that not everyone is going to be wonderfully receptive and instantly appreciative of the help.*
>
> *Some places are easier than others to "remove" people from, so they can join their host families. They*

aren't supposed to just leave. There is paperwork. The Red Cross, like everyone, is overwhelmed. I will have a better feel for that after going to the centers tomorrow.

Steve said the little 4' x 6' area a person has in the shelter is their home for now. It's all they have. The media are exploiting these people through photography and video. It's kind of like taking pictures of people in the slums of Brazil.

Thanks for all you do.

Michael

A SECOND LETTER

Later in the day, Seth sent a second message to the staff...

AIM exists to mobilize and equip the church for missions. Here's what that looks like this week: Michael Paul and Steve Wallace are in Baton Rouge connecting us to needs. Ben and Janeen Messner are taking the 70 AIM interns and staff to Baton Rouge on Wednesday. We'll kick the connecting process into high gear this week.

The Messners will spearhead our organizational effort. This will include projects designed specifically to link the Church up with needs on the ground. Primary needs at present are ministry-related. Clothes and food aren't the problem — brokenness and emotional wounds are the issue. People need ministry. And this is what we at AIM love to do!

Please pray.

God bless you.

Seth

THE PACE QUICKENS

Janeen's Journal:

Today was just a blur. Planning, doing laundry, and packing again for another trip. Ben and I have been living like this for the last year and a half. Our time in Georgia was meant to be restful. We're not objecting to the chance to go to Baton Rouge and help with all this. Just the opposite. I think we're energized by everything.

Tonight Ben, Mark Almand and Seth met for prayer. Everyone agreed the Messners needed to arrive ahead of the AIM intern team to assess the situation. They leave in the morning.

Ben's Journal:

Where is this roller coaster going? What is over the next hill?

"God, go before us we pray."

September 5, 2005

AN UPDATE FROM BATON ROUGE
By now, Michael Paul had another update from Baton Rouge...

I have just returned from the Istrouma Baptist Church, a center with several hundred evacuees. Horribly sad, but a great ministry opportunity. I met and prayed with many.

There was a group from Los Angeles publicly recruiting for 300 evacuees to fly out tonight. Most evacuees were afraid they would manipulate their money from them somehow. So many have fear, anxiety, anger, confusion and simply no trust or peace.

There are just over a dozen Red Cross shelters and about that many more independent shelters (most all of them are churches). New ones open each day. There is definitely no shortage of evacuees. There is definitely much that can be done.

Many evacuees may be reluctant to leave Louisiana. People here are very committed to this state, and especially the New Orleans area. The Cajun culture is very tight. Many in the worst-hit areas (St. Bernard Parish and lower Jefferson Parish) are Cajuns and Creoles, and very few will leave Louisiana.

I am believing huge things from a huge God. Our church attendance this morning was about 25% larger than normal. Worship was deep and very tearful for most. Our interim pastor lost everything — he is a professor at the seminary in New Orleans. The families I am hosting went into the suburbs today to check their houses. They took pictures of the mess. It is bad. They saw dead bodies floating in the water.

May the Lord be merciful to us all.

EXHAUSTION AND FEAR HIT THE STAFF

Fear struck Ben's heart today as he journey toward Louisiana. It is the normal stuff of insecurity and the weight of perceived expectation. He was exhausted. It would have been easier to say "no" to this whole deal. But, he knew that the lives of hundreds of evacuees living in the balance. And 70 AIM interns and AIM staff were expecting them to have their base and ministry set up several days later.

Janeen's Journal:

We finally got on the road for Baton Rouge at 1:30 p.m. We met Ben's brother, Tom, in Birmingham at a fast-food restaurant.

There was a sign taped on the door concerning Katrina evacuees. If they worked for the restaurant, they were supposed to call a special phone number.

We drove the long way there because the better routes were blocked. There were trees down and we saw a fair amount of damage along the way. We stopped frequently for gas.

We pulled into Steve Wallace's driveway close to midnight. He took us to meet Dale and Debbie Cleary, our hosts for the next several days. They were wonderful and waited for us to get there to give us a sweet welcome.

September 6, 2005

Ben's Prayer:

"Jesus, show me how to lead in this effort. Protect my precious wife today and cover our marriage. I need favor in this day as the hours are ticking by until the AIM intern team arrives, expecting us to be set up here."

We arose early to meet with the host church where we will be camping out for the next six days. From that point on the day didn't stop. The days never seemed to stop out there out. Leaders from the River Community Church met with us in the morning and showed us around. One of their members was constructing outside-showers for our group.

GROUND ZERO: THE RIVER CENTER

In the afternoon, we ventured into downtown Baton Rouge to go to the shelter at the River Center that is housing thousands of evacuees. We parked in a garage and had to go down a few flights of stairs to get to the street. The stairwell reeked of urine and it was apparent that people were hanging out there a lot at night.

The place was very tense. The Red Cross volunteers were growing weary and the evacuees were definitely feeling cramped. Children ran everywhere, the walls were plastered with important information and phone numbers, policemen roamed the hallways, and dozens camped outside for smoking opportunities.

The goal for today was to establish an AIM presence in the shelter, so that our AIM intern team can effectively serve there, but also so the "evacuee placement service" can get up and running. We know there are several generous families who want to host these needy people. Our goal is see this start to happen by the end of the day tomorrow.

Walking toward the large building, we noticed many police officers but still had a feeling of danger. There were homeless people wandering all around. A good portion seemed like they were ready to start a fight with anyone who even looked at them the wrong way. We knew we'd be hostile, too, if we had just lost everything.

No one felt at rest in that environment. The police didn't help us feel safe either. Ben didn't wear a uniform or a badge, and he didn't carry a gun, but Janeen just wanted to stay close to him anyway. The lack of safety was all too familiar to their time in Africa where they had been robbed seven times in one year.

We waited in a small line to get into the River Center. Scattered Red Cross volunteers looked like they were frantically involved in whatever they were doing and could not be interrupted. We found out where to go, walked up the broken escalator and met some very tired volunteers sitting behind a desk. We signed in and they gave us badges with our names written on them.

Ben let them know that AIM had a bigger group that could begin helping on Friday morning and continue until Tuesday morning. Food preparation and serving meals seemed to be a great need, so we committed to help with breakfast and lunch for those days.

Before leaving, Ben and Janeen stepped into the sleeping area and explained to some other volunteers that we were also offering to help place evacuees in homes around the U.S. We made a good contact, a woman named Debra.

It was so hard to figure out where to start, physically or spiritually. The first step was praying for a spirit of peace to fall on the shelters.

Janeen's Journal:
The family hosting us is amazing and their home is beautiful. I feel like this is God blessing us today. He knew our needs and provided for them.

It took us awhile to get back to where we were staying because of the traffic. When we arrived, the

Cleary family shared their dinner with us. They told us about some of what they learned in the shelters where they volunteered. One thing was emphasized: the need for childcare and activities for kids.

"BRING YOUR PEOPLE IN HERE"

Steve Wallace, associate pastor of River Community Church in Baton Rouge, gave us a little tidbit that indicated the level of humane, moral and spiritual health that is beginning to rise up. Yesterday, during an open share time, one of the elders at his church — a man whose company is a major international construction/development firm — shared that many of the needs for emergency, commercial real-estate space were being addressed in an astonishing way.

Baton Rouge-area businesses are opening their offices so that their New Orleans competitors have space to operate and stay in business.

"Bring your people in here. We'll make space, so you can make a living." Law firms. Accounting firms. Developers. Medical professionals.

"If a brother or sister is without clothing and in need of daily food, and one of you says to them, 'Go in peace, be warmed and be filled,' and yet you do not give them what is necessary for their body, what use is that?" (James 2:15-16)

September 7, 2005

Dale Cleary, the Messner's host, traveled around with our small staff today. This was a divine appointment because he was able to open doors for our team to minister that seemed to be impossibly closed. The Red Cross is in control here. They are rightfully concerned about who gets into the shelters, but Dale worked out every hindrance.

The AIM intern team is now set up to serve in three different shelters: River Center, Istrouma Baptist Church Shelter, and one in Livingston, LA. Opportunities include serving meals, organizing kid's activities, counseling evacuees, cleaning up garbage, sorting through supplies and distributing them.

Our days will start early to avoid the horrible traffic. Baton Rouge has doubled in population. The roads were only designed one-third of the amount of people that are here. It can take hours to go just a few miles. We are impressed by the good attitudes people continue to extend.

BACK TO THE RIVER CENTER

Ben and Janeen decided to check in again at the River Center. Steve Wallace drove them there. It was a completely different place than it was 24 hours before, both in terms of security and order. The National Guard now had a presence and was covering the place with guards. The Red Cross also seemed more organized. Amazing how quickly everything adapted to the needs of this crisis situation.

A pattern quickly revealed itself in regards to shelter life. The mornings and early afternoons would be very orderly and peaceful. The National Guard and Red Cross workers all were at carefully selected stations and kept strong control of their areas. But by the afternoon of each day chaos would settle in again as NG or RC would respond to needs and no one would take their place. And then around 8:00 PM things would begin to calm down again as people prepared for bed.

We connected with Debra, their contact at the River Center, and wanted to try the database out, since so many evacuees were inquiring with Debra about housing options. The only problem was that they did not have a printout of the database with them and they could not access the web from there to print it out.

Ben Messner:

There is no sense of organization here. The shelters do not have wireless access and getting my phone to work is a chore. I spend all day in the shelters and then spend most of my night trying to catch up on the work generated by the home office. I know there is a brilliant database with all the information I need but I can't access it during the day. I need a printed copy now!

Steve drove back to the church where we printed out about 100 files, as many as we had time for, from the database. It was a start. We drove back and Debra cleared a space for us to sit by her at the table. People lined up to talk to us about the locations we had where people were opening their homes.

A woman named Simone came up to us and introduced herself. She was a tremendous help on that chaotic day, then we never saw her again. She was an evacuee herself who decided she needed to get up and do something to help. Debra also was an evacuee from the Ninth Ward, which is likely the most hardcore neighborhood in New Orleans. She kept saying to the evacuees as they came to our placement table, "I'm from the Lower Nine; I ain't afraid of dyin."

As we sat at the placement table we would listen to people's situations and asked where they wanted to relocate. A road atlas was very helpful so we could see where the host families lived in relation to big cities and areas that evacuees were looking to go. We made calls once we thought we found good fits. Some of the hosts were ready to pick up the evacuees anytime, while others were hesitant about the reality of people coming to stay.

There was hesitation on both sides. Many of the evacuees we spoke with never came back once we started setting things up. They were afraid of going somewhere else and living with strangers — just as the host families were afraid it may not work out for them either.

Janeen's Journal:

That evening we left to go to the airport to pick up some friends who were going to help us with the database. It was great to see familiar faces again. That's what the evacuees needed, too, I thought — something familiar.

September 8, 2005

That morning we were a small army, if you can call four an army, of all "database people" at the River Center. We gave a quick lesson on matching and placing people with host families. They began helping as soon as they sat down at the table.

We found more people who needed help with transportation than housing. Most people had a place to go, but no way to get there. We helped as much as we could.

OUR FIRST MIRACLE- TYANKA

About halfway through the day, a woman named Tyanka came to Janeen, explaining that it was urgent for her to get her mother and child out of the shelter as soon as possible. Her mother had diabetes and was not doing well. She was healthy before Katrina, but now she was hitting some bad highs and lows and, being in the shelter, she wasn't getting the medical attention necessary. Tyanka feared her mother could die soon.

Janeen asked Tyanka where she wanted to go. She said that she had a friend in Corpus Christi, Texas, and she knew that evacuees were getting better care there as well. Janeen looked up some names on the database for that area, but the closest match she found was a family in Harlingen.

Their names were Cesar and Jennifer Gonzalez. They work for AIM! (Is that cool or what?) We called and explained Tyanka's situation. They were willing to help in any way, including transportation. They worked on borrowing a van, so that they could come and get the family in Baton Rouge and drive them to Corpus Christi. (That's a 1,250 mile round-trip.)

Tyanka told Janeen she would come back to check in later. Janeen heard of a bus leaving for Houston around 5 p.m. and thought that it would work out great if Tyanka and her family could get on that bus. That way, Cesar and Jennifer could meet her in Houston, rather than driving all the way to Baton Rouge. Janeen called Cesar. He really liked that plan and was hoping it would work.

Janeen searched all around the shelter like a maniac the next couple of hours in hopes of finding Tyanka. Janeen had her paged on the speakers. She couldn't find her, but we signed her up for seats on the bus, along with her mother and her son, in hopes that we could get to them in time.

We had nearly given up on getting them on that bus. The area out front where it was parked was jammed with people. Some passengers were already aboard and others were ready to get on when we spotted Tyanka. Janeen grabbed her and asked her if she could get ready to go in time. She said she would try and took off running.

It was like an obstacle course. She called the caterer for the shelter. (They owed her money for working in the kitchen from the past few days). The caterer was running the check over to the River Center while Tyanka was getting her mom ready to go. Her mom obviously had a low sugar level when all this was happening.

On top of everything else, two movie stars were walking around the shelter causing little clouds of chaos. In the middle of everything with Tyanka, it was great to look over and see these famous people picking kids up and helping give them a smile.

The bus was waiting on Tyanka. It had been about thirty minutes and the check was still not there. We promised to send it if we could meet the person who had it. We ran through the shelter and found the man we needed to go to for the check. We memorized his face and ran back to her cot. We loaded up and carted the remnants of their things to the bus.

Tyanka was trying to keep her son and mom on track while we attempted to get everything they had into the back of the bus. We could not believe that this was actually working out! We exchanged hugs and the bus embarked on the adventure to the Astrodome, with Tyanka's family.

Before she left, we gave her a sign that had "Cesar Gonzalez" written on it, so that she would have a way of finding him once she arrived in Houston. It was a miracle so far, but we knew it would take another miracle for Cesar and Jennifer to find Tyanka at the Astrodome. We were so busy we only had time to pray for one miracle at a time.

As we closed up our table for the day, we were exhausted. We were expecting the AIM interns to arrive late that night, but we got a call saying that due to the newly enforced curfew, some of them would stay at one of the stops until morning.

THE TROOPS ARRIVE

Ben sent out another e-mail:

We learned again today that it is incredibly important to establish a relationship with the evacuees prior to them being willing to trust you with a relocation of their lives. The best candidates for the housing program take more time to process the decision, which is a good thing in our minds.

An awesome man from Kentucky spent the entire day visiting with people, offering them a ride and housing at his home. NO ONE took the offer! As we build relationships, continue to pray for us.

The AIM intern team arrives soon, which will be great. They will dive into serving in a few select shelters by serving meals, playing with kids, and praying with evacuees. Continue to keep them in your prayers.

We ask for your continued patience in this process. Please understand that not every host family will end up with an evacuee family. Many want to stay in the South. In the end, God's plan will be accomplished. My theme continues to be "let the Church arise and be the bride she was created to be"...thus far, that is happening.

ALLI ARRIVES

Alli Mellon has devoted her life to the Lord's work. She leads mission trips all over the world for AIM. In her "spare time," she is a professional songwriter. Alli drove the AIM interns to Baton Rouge.

<u>Alli Mellon, AIM Staff:</u>

We were filled with anticipation as we drove into downtown Baton Rouge. It was just after sunrise. Eleven days earlier Hurricane Katrina pummeled our Gulf coastline.

It was ten days after the levee in Louisiana broke, flooding us with more tragedy than a weather-born storm had ever driven home before — complete with pictures that those of us who were safe and dry could barely comprehend. Mothers cradling babies, crying for help from rooftops. The now-homeless walking down Interstates toting their precious few possessions in garbage bags. The symbolism was stark. Treasures in garbage bags. Things change. Overnight. Or, as God puts it, "Do not boast about tomorrow, for you do not know what a day may bring about."

AIM interns are not your run-of-the-mill teenagers and young adults. They are devoted Christians who have committed between four months and one year of their lives to make a difference in the world. These folks were on their way to such places as New Zealand, Kenya, South Africa, Swaziland and Mexico. Just three days before, they didn't have the faintest idea that they'd be driving into the storm zone, passing road signs knocked over like dominoes and twisted by 165 mile-an-hour winds. Seeing metal crushed under the boot heel of Katrina like aluminum cans. Mourning the proud Southern Oaks, now fallen firewood beside the road.

CHANGE OF PLANS

The email sent out by Ben saying, "Change of plans" was welcomed with an "amen" by many AIM interns. However, some of the AIM interns never even got the warning. The plans had changed so quickly to relocate the AIM intern training camp to Baton Rouge that some of the AIM intern's did not even know about it. They didn't have a clue, until they arrived from all over America and Canada, that they were going to Louisiana. It was a bigger surprise for some than others...

Jessica Alaniz, AIM intern
Michigan

Going to Baton Rouge was a challenging, stretching, awesome experience. I will never forget it! I'm from Michigan. At home, I was watching the hurricane story on the news. My heart really went out to the people. I was so sad, but honestly hoped I would never have to see people in that situation face to face. Even at home, I knew that would be hard.

I got on my flight from Detroit to Atlanta. When I landed, I got my luggage and found the spot where the AIM group was. Someone there asked me if I had a bag packed for Baton Rouge. I looked at them very confused and told them, "I'm going to Mexico." It was then, in the Atlanta airport, that I found out I was going to Baton Rouge. My first reaction was shock and dread. I instantly thought to myself that I really didn't want to go. But, I didn't say anything and I went. The first day there, I wasn't over not wanting to be there. But that changed.

Instead of complaining about the change of venue, however, the attitudes were overwhelmingly positive. After one night in Georgia, where they slept in army tents and used homemade toilets in the woods, they had piled onto vans and buses for the long trek to

Louisiana. Kayla, the Kenya Resident Advisor, led her team in a prayer ride in which they prayed for each state they drove through, the situation they were going into and all of those affected by the hurricane.

As the team traveled, they spent time alone with the Lord, asking for God's direction and strength to minister to the hurting. They also asked each other "get-to-know-you" questions, laughing like old friends at each other's middle names! Only a few short waking hours before, they were strangers to each other. Quickly, everyone sensed it was important to learn each other's strengths before heading into battle together.

AN UNEXPECTED STOP

Driving across Georgia, Alabama, and Mississippi took longer than expected. The AIM interns and their RAs crashed on a cold, bare gym floor for just a few hours, most of them without a blanket or pillow. As Alli watched them doing their best to get comfortable on that gym floor, she knew that this was a special group of kids. So far in this adventure in missions, they had been unexpectedly taken to another state and were now spending the most uncomfortable night ever!

Very few of us got much sleep but we piled back onto the vehicles and continued our journey. Three short hours later, we were at River Community Church, in the Baton Rouge suburb of Prairieville. Most kids would have wanted to take a shower, catch a long nap and change clothes. They simply ran inside to grab breakfast – a muffin. Soon, we were driving into downtown Baton Rouge for our first day of ministry.

We couldn't help but wonder how everyone would respond to what they were about to experience...

Chris McArthur, AIM intern
Mississippi

When Hurricane Katrina hit on August 29, I experienced it. I was about an hour-and-a half from the coast. I was without power, running water or a working phonefor over a week. Toward the end of that week, I had to leave my hot, dry home to go to Gainesville.

I felt awful for leaving my home and church to come to a place that had power, air-conditioning and running water. I felt a need to be back home to help in the community.

When I arrived, I found out that we would be going to Baton Rouge, LA to help with the relief there. I had to prepare myself for facing Katrina once more. This excited me very much. I knew that God could use me to care for people facing such pain.

I saw people who were desperate for a change of clothes, because they were still wearing the ones they were wearing when they were rescued. I saw people who were so distressed that they could not even remember how to smile. I saw families turn against each other. They were so stressed out! I saw people who found a glimpse of hope from a simple smile. I saw people who needed to be heard but had no one to turn to.

These people needed more than a bottle of water. They needed to know that they matter. They needed to know that there is hope.

Justin O'Hara, AIM intern
Arizona

Usually I am the one watching all the disasters unfold on TV. I watched Katrina happen and treated it like every other disaster I had ever seen. I was sad to see it happen and wanted to help, but I live in Tucson, Arizona and I didn't feel like I could do anything.

Besides, I was going to Atlanta for a week to prepare myself for a mission adventure in Kenya. But, I prayed to God to work on the hearts of the people at AIM to see that Louisiana needed our help. I prayed for a week and

God answered my prayer. I got an e-mail saying that training camp was moving to Baton Rouge! That was so cool. I had a chance to actually do something.

What I saw when I got there was beyond belief. Huge trees snapped in half, like tooth picks. Billboard signs bent over and mangled like chicken wire, the stench of the river becoming overwhelming in some places. Lone houses barely standing, in neighborhoods which used to thrive. Boats on dry land and "dry land" under twelve feet of water. The towns, by sight, seemed forever lost in chaos.

What would we see inside the shelters? Roads and houses and bridges and levees and cities can be rebuilt. Trees can be replanted. Can dreams be brought back to life? How would we be able to bring hope to the hurting? How could we show them that God is still with us — even in tragedy?

September 9, 2005

The team arrived in two groups during the night, one at 2:00 a.m and the other at 5:45 a.m. The first group had no luggage. It was all with the group that arrived later. They slept on the church floor without bedding. Ben only slept for 1 hour. He had been up for nearly 46 hours straight. That redefines exhaustion.

That first morning, we thanked God for leading the Messners to leave Gainesville and arrive in Baton Rouge earlier than we originally planned - even before the Military Police arrived. Janeen was a pro at navigating the Center's back alleyways and loading docks. She helped everyone get registered with the Red Cross and where to report for duty.

> <u>Janeen's Journal:</u>
>
> *The morning was crazy. We ended up being thirty minutes late because of traffic, but everyone jumped into serving as fast as they could get their Red Cross badges taped on.*
>
> *Physically, I constantly felt like I was going to lose my balance and fall over. My equilibrium felt messed up and my body temperature was going up and down. I was in a strange zone like this until the next day. I wanted to slow down but I was determined to push myself because there were so many things at the shelter that I was in the middle of working on.*
>
> *Finally, I picked up Tyanka's check. She'll be so happy to get it.*

DAY ONE IN THE SHELTERS FOR THE AIM INTERNS

The number of people in the shelter immediately overwhelmed the group that served in the River Center. It is hard to imagine the number 5,000 until you are there in the midst of it. There was very little conversation among us as we took it all in. The time was around 7:00 in the morning.

Picture thousands of cots, lined up side by side, covering every available floor surface in both the arena and the huge convention center area. Soft lights were turned down low, but it was still too much for those accustomed to sleeping in the secure darkness of home, and too little for those unsure and feeling unsafe.

Survivors. The word hit us like a brick. If God has spared us, doesn't He have a plan for us? A reason to survive? Hope rebounded our hearts.

We waded into the depths of the Center. Babies cried from darkened corners. The smell of urine filled the room. Nobody was moving. They were frozen by grief.

Our first task was to prepare and serve breakfast to the masses...

We found the two kitchens located in the shelter. Some of us got right to work setting out breakfast pastries, and some of the AIM interns mastered the system of packaging 5,000 box lunches for later in the day. Jessica from the Mexico team quickly learned the ropes and led the crew. Everyone quickly jumped into doing various jobs, from sorting clothes in the Distribution Room to stacking packs of diapers neatly against a wall.

Bethany Marron, AIM AIM intern
Rhode Island

The opportunity to serve God's people in Baton Rouge truly blessed and challenged my relationship with the Lord. After five days of watching the news reports and reading of the inhumane conditions in New Orleans, I was forced to leave the comforts of my Rhode Island living room. I headed to AIM headquarters to volunteer for work in Baton Rouge, LA.

After a seemingly endless ride on a bus with students from all over the country, we arrived in Baton Rouge and reported to the River Center. The first day of work seemed surreal. I was excited to be meeting an immediate need and though thoroughly exhausted managed to serve breakfast, sanitize hands, and organize supplies with an enthusiastic attitude. I watched people that day; I observed as school age children ran around with seemingly no supervision and the elderly remained confined to their uncomfortable army cots. Young men and women walked around with a single plastic bag full of possessions. Families formed makeshift borders to their living areas with convention center chairs.

Even though we had no sleep last night, we went into the shelters immediately. The team served with such energy and humble hearts. The military and Red Cross seemed to be impressed. The team could not believe the things they witnessed. This is the perfect grounds for ministry training.

LESSONS LEARNED

We learned some lessons today:

1. If someone assigns a task to you, you must complete it.

2. Do not allow yourself to be stolen away by someone else who needs you!

3. If you <u>do</u>, you will get chewed out by the shelter manager.

4. Wash your hands continually with anti-bacterial soap. The chance of disease and sickness is huge.

5. Smile. People need smiles.

6. No task is too small. There seems to be a competition between different groups here, so we informed our group to do any task asked of us no matter how small.

PASTOR JIM'S STORY

By this time people willing to host evacuees were tired of waiting. Many took it upon themselves to drive to Baton Rouge unannounced to find evacuees to go home with them. Jim, a man from Kentucky, was just a fellow. Most came thinking evacuees would simply jump in the truck with them and they would return to their homes right away. This rarely happened. So many returned home with no one because they were unwilling to stay overnight in the shelter. This was not the case with Jim.

All his attempts on the first day to get evacuees out of the shelter failed, but he stayed and built several relationships. Many people gratefully considered his offer but no one took it. Finally, at the end of the third day, Jim found a few people willing to live with him. His perseverance paid off. He lived in the shelter for three days among the people and modeled Christ to them. Finally, a few evacuees trusted him enough to leave with him.

BACK TO THE AIM INTERNS

The rest of the crew went out to build new relationships at other shelters. Led by Dan Cleary, they had incredible success at getting into some key shelters. God opened doors that seemed to be completely locked at first. The relocation service, plus ministry activities, will roll out at these two new locations starting on Saturday. So many hours have been poured into this so far and so few were placed.

Ben's Journal

The host families are so demanding at times. We keep getting pressure to find them an evacuee now! They signed up on the database and so they expect immediate service. Those people have no idea how long this process takes. I wish more were like Jim who came and lived among the evacuees to earn their trust. We are not here to serve the host families, rather we are here to serve the evacuees. I need to stay humble and not get angry.

The Baton Rouge crew is pouring out their hearts. Three staff went to manage relocation at a shelter. No one was there to serve meals, so they ended up serving lunch instead. We're trying to follow the Lord. That means letting Him set our agendas. The process will likely improve over the next week. Evacuees are extremely unwilling to move until they receive their paychecks, ID cards, Food Stamp cards and the other services they're waiting for. There's also the trust factor we're still trying to establish. With God, all things are possible.

The frenetic pace didn't slow down over the next 96 hours. But, the team got better and better. They seemed to want to get in just one more conversation with an evacuee they now called "friend." The Lord was beginning to answer our questions about how we could help here. He was beginning to speak to us, and every sentence He spoke had words like "relationship" and "listen" and "care" and "give" in it.

RELATIONSHIPS CAME SLOWLY

Sometimes starting to build relationships wasn't easy...

<u>Jill Blackburn, AIM intern</u>
<u>Mississippi</u>

Though the vast majority of evacuees were extremely grateful for our help, one woman God placed in my path was full of bitterness and hate. She demanded that I bring her specific clothes from the donated ones and get her prescription filled. My initial reaction was to quickly deny her request, and tell her exactly how I felt about her ungrateful demands.

Gently, though, Jesus reminded me of his awesome sacrifice and humility on the cross — the perfect example of the love that we are supposed to show others in His

name. Philippians 2:5-8, "Your attitude should be the
same as that of Christ Jesus: Who, being in the very
nature God, did not consider equality with God something
to be grasped, but made Himself nothing, taking the very
nature of a servant, being made in human likeness. And
being found in appearance as a man, He humbled Himself
and became obedient to death – even death on a cross!"

I humbled myself and did as the lady asked of me. I put myself in her shoes.

NO QUITTERS HERE

In most groups, there are one or two individuals who aren't up to the task. Somebody complaining just a little bit, somebody with sore feet or somebody just "not into" the ministry we are doing. But this group was unique. Everywhere around the huge facility, they were pouring their hearts into the job. Someone commented, "Honestly, I have never seen people work as hard or love as gently. There are no quitters here!"

It was all about relationships. Truth spoken from the mouth of God and poured out onto broken people, through our ears as we silently listened to their stories, through our tears as we knelt beside cots and wheelchairs. Tears that said what we couldn't say with words. Tears that popped up unexpectedly and frequently.

Bonds formed and our names were called out by our new friends as we crossed the Center a hundred times a day in our various tasks. God in us was caring for those who so desperately needed it. There was nothing we could have said, nothing we could have done to put a Band-Aid on the wounded here at the shelters. God did it through us with His healing power. Through His strength and our weakness.

THEN ANOTHER MIRACLE HAPPENED

Before we even walked into the River Center, there was a picture of a man who was missing. His name was Freddie. His parents were staying in the River Center. Our group had been discussing how sad it would be to lose a child, even if that child was an adult. An AIM intern named Shelley prayed for Freddie as she walked by the sign.

As a precaution from disease, the Red Cross stationed people at the entrance to the main room and gave them hand sanitizer to squirt into people's hands. Shelley got the privilege of the hand sanitizing on Sunday. The main room had several thousand people in it, so it was difficult to recognize the people who came in and out. There was one woman, though, who Shelley prayed for every time she came in the door. She didn't know exactly what was wrong, but she could tell something was on her heart. The woman wouldn't accept the sanitizer and looked down as she walked. Shelley left the River Center later that day, not expecting what the next day would bring.

The second morning, Shelley was asked to be at the announcer's table for the day. She gladly accepted because she was there to serve the needs of others, even though she had no idea what the announcer was supposed to do. It turned out that the "announcer's table" was simply a fold-out table and chairs with a sound system and microphone hooked up near it. The announcers would say things over the loud-speakers like, "a chapel service will be held in the so-and-so room at 10:00 this morning" and "anyone needing to meet with FEMA can now do so on the second floor."

Shelley was constantly bombarded with questions that she couldn't answer. She felt so helpless. Through the many announcements and questions of the day, Shelley became stressed. Shelley prayed that God would take the tension away. Five minutes later, the sad woman who'd refused the hand sanitizer the day before came up to the announcer's table. She hugged me and told me she had found her son!

She was overjoyed and couldn't stop jumping around. Shelley was totally excited because, although she does not have children, she knows the pain of losing someone she loves. Shelley asked what the woman's son's name was, so she could pray for her and her son. His name was Freddie! He was the one on the posters that were taped up everywhere. The exact Freddie my team had prayed for the day before! Shelley was in awe. God is good!

GOD STILL SPEAKS

If ever we wondered if God had abandoned His children, we saw constant reminders that He <u>never</u> forsakes His own.

AIM intern Journal:

The hopefulness of Hurricane Katrina survivors absolutely blew me away. One man, whose name I do not remember, told me the story of how he and his wife had gotten out. This was an older couple (probably in their 60s) and had just purchased a new home one year ago, in New Orleans.

When the initial evacuation was issued before the storm hit, the husband would not listen and stayed at his new house while his wife left to stay with a friend outside of the city. That night while the husband was home alone, he believes Jesus spoke to him clearly and boldly. He said, "You need to leave right away!" After hearing this, the husband left to join his wife.

That night the levee broke, the city was flooded and the couple's house was destroyed. The couple was evacuated from the city in time and survived — though their house and all their possessions did not. As I listened to him tell his story all he could say was, "Let me show you how good God is!"

He was so hopeful and so thankful that God had rescued him from the disaster. I asked the man if he had lost any of his family. He told me that he had and that he was trying to relocate them. I was completely blown away and humbled by how much hope he had — everything he had ever known was destroyed and he wanted to tell me how good God was.

EVACUEES HELPING EVACUEES

Our perceptions were becoming scrambled. Extremes became the norm. The homeless endured storms of every sort. Some evacuees found a loved one. Others learned that a loved one was missing or swept away. The relief centers felt like field hospitals outside a war zone. A few responded with anger. More than one responded by taking care of others...

Lindsay Vos, AIM intern
Iowa

I was sitting outside the women's bathroom dispensing the unending supply of hand sanitizer, when I noticed a woman sitting in the cot nearest to me. I continued to do my job as I watched her out of the corner of my eye. To my surprise, she began to care for a very sick man next to her.

It seemed so out of place that in this desolate, hopeless place that this woman would reach out her hand and wipe the nose of an ungrateful, broken man. My mind was made up right then that I had to get to know this amazing woman.

I turned, reached out my hand and said, "I'm Lindsay." There was something almost electric in her eyes as she lifted her gaze to meet mine. She introduced herself as Anne, and immediately began to tell me about her life.

She was divorced and proud of it. I have never received a more stern "stay away from boys" talk. After a few minutes of conversation, I mustered the courage to ask her about the ill-looking man lying on the cot next to her. She then began to explain that he was her little brother who suffered from autism. Now he had a severe flu. It turns out that she worked with special-needs chil-

dren. "It's them normal kids I can't stand!" She told me of how God had placed that gift on her heart.

I asked her about her experience with the hurricane. I carefully tested the waters by asking how long she had been at the River Center. I was surprised to hear that she was one of the first ones there, and she had lost track of the days.

Anne told of how she knew full well that the storm was arriving, but she refused to set foot out of her house until she had finished preparing and eating her fried chicken dinner. She laughed heartily about it as if it was a fond memory of years past. I complimented her good cheer, and she said it was all because of her "Maries."

I was confused at first, but was enlightened when she gently lifted a rosary that was tucked beneath her pillow. Now I'm not Catholic, but I asked her to pray with me anyway. Anne prayed for a new home and for her brother's health. I prayed the most thankful prayer I ever had. I thanked God for this hopeful woman who had remained strong and seemingly untouched by such a crippling disaster.

Ryan Amstutz, an AIM intern from Ohio, wrote this in his journal:

Every day the shelter staff had volunteers come in to sort clothes, "shop" for families and do other physical work along with us.

One individual there impacted my life so much. His name is Emmanuel. He was tall, and probably about 50 years old and he was one of the volunteers. The first day I arrived, he was there sorting clothes and I was shopping for the evacuees. Every time I came into the room where he was working he would look up and just say something *encouraging like, "You're doing great!"*

This continued every day and I began to look forward to seeing him. I realized that I wasn't the only one that he did this to. Every time I saw him he was encouraging someone, joking with them, helping them out and just letting everyone know his excitement that he could help out.

Later, I found out his story. Emmanuel was an evacuee himself. I'm not sure if he had any family or if he had lost his family. The important thing to him was that no matter what he had lost or how he felt he was there showing Christ's love to volunteers and evacuees alike.

It was hard to leave after working with him all week. I considered him to be an angel in the midst of a lot of depression. I want to be like him.

HUMOR IN THE MIDST OF GREAT PAIN

Keith Barkman, AIM intern
Canada

After the hurricane, most of the survivors worried about their own families and whether or not they were alive. One lady I met wasn't only thinking about her family, but of starting new relationships.

I was handing out personal hygiene and beauty products when I stumbled upon an 83-year-old woman. She was sitting on her cot and I asked her if she would like a small amount of Mary Kay perfume. She accepted it and then told me that the perfume would help her attract a man that she was looking at!

This short conversation helped to break the tension that covered the arena at the River Center. I realized that even though life was put on hold because of the hurri-

cane, this wasn't "the end" for the survivors. There is always a rainbow at the end of the storm.

THE END OF THE FIRST DAY

Life would go on. It would be different — even unwelcome to a few — but life would go on. We were there to encourage these beautiful people to go on. And no one had to go on alone. They could go with Jesus Christ. Through the relationships He gave us, we began to see Him in a new way.

He is the Way. He is the Way home for family members scattered by the waves and water, filling stadium floors, alone. He is the Way back for brothers and mothers separated from one another, searching thousands of posters that cover every wall, longing to see that one they seek. He is the Way for those who hear bad news, as well.

He is the Truth. He is the Truth that promises never to leave us or forsake us, even when all seems lost and forsaken. He is the Truth that can't be ripped from our arms by 165 mph winds, or forced underwater when a levee breaks.

And, He is the Life. He is the Life that is breathed into us in the midst of despair. Underneath the covers of a shelter cot. Through the tears that drip onto used clothing when no one else is watching. He is the life that lives on inside of us, even after we've watched futures dashed and dreams die.

He is the way, the truth, and the life. That's the message of hope we brought with us to the River Center the very first morning we arrived. When we left at the end of our day, we had experienced that hope as we never had before. Never before had we been so convinced that, without Jesus, life is nothing but a broken levee, a drowned dream and a muddy future.

It was hard to walk out of the shelter, and drive "home" to our makeshift camp. None of us were ready to leave. We knew that when we did go, we would leave a lot of lonely people sitting on cots, waiting for a reason to smile again. We couldn't wait to come back the next day.

<u>Janeen's Journal:</u>

Before going to sleep, I read Psalm 57:1, "Have mercy on me, O God, have mercy on me, for in You my soul takes refuge. I will take refuge in the shadow of your wings until the disaster has passed."

This spoke to me and carried me through the rest of my time in Baton Rouge.

September 10, 2005

As we returned to the shelters for our second day of service, we had no expectations of "take two aspirin, rest, drink plenty of liquids and you'll be fine." We had met the people living inside. We knew many of their names. The first day we were at the shelter, people had huddled under their blankets for most of the day, not seeing a reason to get out of their cots. On our second day there, the people were starting to stir. A newly revived tension, silenced the day before only by exhaustion, could be heard in loud voices in the hall, in desperate pleas for help that looked like wouldn't ever arrive...

First Presbyterian Church in downtown Baton Rouge had planned a major event just outside the River Center for the kids. They asked our group to help. Throughout the day we organized basketball games, cooked burgers and hotdogs, monitored the railroad tracks, painted faces, played with kids and loved on people. The event was a major success.

Alli Melon:
From the River Center hurricane shelter in Baton Rouge:

Heartbreak and hope like I saw on the faces today can hardly be described in words. This morning I sat down on the floor to play with two small kids who were basically caring for themselves while their mother went looking for help. Dwayne and David were three and four years old, respectively.

Seeing the Red Cross badge on my chest, a four-year-old girl from a neighboring cot came running up to me. She grabbed my shirt and earnestly scanned my face. "Have you found my sister? Have you found my sister?" Her eyes begged for a "YES!"

As I told her, "No, I haven't found your sister," my eyes filled with tears. The little girl's sister had been lost in the storm. I wasn't able to give her the answer she desperately longed to hear, but I was able to share with her about a big God who had brought her safely out of the storm.

"My mama got wet," she told me. I said, "I know she got wet, but you know what? God brought her here. He has big plans for her, and for you."

I prayed that her sister would be found alive. My words sounded so small in the midst of that room full of hurting people, but our God remained a big God. The little girl seemed to find comfort in those words, and she sat down to play with us as only a child can.

Our hearts joined with those who were crying out to God on behalf of their loved ones. We cried out for them, too.

The longer we were at the shelters, we focused less on the pastries we were handing out and more on the people who were eating them. The team paused to look people in the eye and ask them if they'd like orange or apple juice. They sang praise songs to God as they served in the three-hour meal lines, working shoulder-to-shoulder with about one hundred Scientology, atheist, and agnostic volunteers.

Even as the tension grew among those living in the shelters, joy grew among our young people. They walked the floor, asking the Lord who He would have them talk to and what He would have them say. They asked Jesus to speak to them and give them words for these hurting hearts. By now, we were all confident that we were not there to preach sermons on how "God's gonna make everything ok." We were there to listen to the people as they sat in the middle of a world that was definitely "not ok."

Andrea Metzler, AIM intern
Iowa

I was sitting right outside a women's restroom on

hand sanitizer patrol.

I looked around the huge room. I wanted to talk to people, hear their stories, share in their pains but I was nervous. What would I say? So I continued to sit, squirting sanitizer in hand after hand.

• Those fortunate enough to have their families with them clustered together, making little cot islands among the chaos. Others were alone, curled up in their beds, perhaps not wanting to face another day in this hopeless, lonely place.

A little boy came up to me, wanting more sanitizer, I kept telling him, "no more, no more" but he persisted.

Suddenly I heard a woman's voice say, "Your momma's calling you, boy. Go find your momma!" I turned around and saw the smiling face of an older African-American woman.

"I'm glad you didn't give that boy no more sanitizer," she said. "You gotta be firm with these kids."

I laughed and asked her name. "Margaret, from New Orleans." For the next 40 minutes, she told me all about her cozy neighborhood in New Orleans. It was one of those neighborhoods where everyone knows everyone else. Neighbors gathered together at the local café to chat. You could walk down the street and see people relating to one another on their porches. Everyone waved hello to each other. No one ever locked the doors.

"It was such a nice neighborhood, and now it's all underwater." Margaret told me about her beautiful garden and her library of medical books. "Such a shame, all those books, gone."

Margaret was in the middle of cooking dinner when her sister called to make sure she was getting ready to leave before the hurricane hit. She made her way to the

Super Dome, thinking she'd be back in her kitchen before too long. "I remember saying to my sister, 'I forgot to rake my leaves. I'll have to do that when I get back.'"

But, Margaret would not be going back home. After the hurricane hit, she was able to get on the first bus out of New Orleans. That bus took her to the River Center in Baton Rouge, where I met her.

"Nobody cries in public. They want to look strong but they all go off and cry alone." I could hear the sadness in her voice as she told me that she had no idea what's next for her, no idea where her next Christmas will be.

In the midst of all this uncertainty, Margaret had one thing to hold onto, "Jesus is faithful, He's taking care of me," she said to me. We prayed together. I know that no matter where she ends up, Jesus will always be taking care of her.

I had asked God to give me the courage to talk to someone, and He answered my prayers in Margaret!

On this second day, Margaret was not the only one who had suffered the loss of everything...

<u>Kelsey Manfredi, AIM intern</u>
<u>Virginia</u>

When we first arrived at the River Center, the first light of day was starting to illuminate the entrance. I was greeted by tired, friendly faced MPs who seemed surprised to have been deployed to guard and secure a refugee camp located in Louisiana!

I have been to the slums of Ecuador, the migrant villages of Mexico and the drug-infested government housing in Washington DC, but the despair I saw in those places differed from the sadness I sensed emanating from these people. The total and utter destruction and loss of their houses, their communities and their very way of life caused my heart to hurt, too!

The auditorium, which had now become both bedrooms and living rooms for over 5,000 homeless Americans, was beginning to stir. Babies toddled out of their beds and there was an odd rustling sound as 5,000 people dressed in near silence.

I took a prayer walk around the auditorium and felt led to sit and talk with a woman who was watching an adorable curly haired baby. The woman was Deborah, and the baby was her grandson, Jonathan. I asked if she would tell me her story. She was a fellow believer and a resident of New Orleans.

Her house and all her belongings had been submerged under water for over two weeks. We talked about the effects of losing such things as memorable jewelry and priceless photographs. We talked about how it was to attempt to sleep in a room swimming with the constant movements of so many people, to bathe in a shower con-structed on the street guarded by gun-toting MPs, and how it felt to ask people you have never met for such essentials as underwear and deodorant.

I was touched by her peace and her determination to go on. As I was leaving, I asked her if she had any prayer requests. It wasn't until then that she told me that one of her children, her son Darrell, was still missing!

I was taken aback — she had a precious son and she didn't know where he was! He might have been hurt. Or worse, dead. Yet here she was telling me, the "mission-ary," of the provisions and protection of God! It was one of the few times in my life that I have truly witnessed the peace of God — a peace that surpasses all under-standing!

I talked with and encouraged Deborah, but there was still no word about the whereabouts of Darrell. Deborah thanked me for my attention and concern and gave me a goodbye hug. She is going to e-mail me when she finds out any news of her son.

A great tragedy has happened in Louisiana, Mississippi, and Alabama. Yet, it is also true that God is raising up men and women in the midst of that suffering who exemplify His supernatural peace. We can encourage our world with the reality of God, and tell them of His promise to uphold and strengthen any of His children who find themselves "walking through the valley of the shadow of death."

REASON TO CELEBRATE

So much loss. So much uncertainty. But in the midst of it...

Lisa Hardy, AIM intern
Texas

On my second day at the shelter at River Center, I was walking through the room telling families that there was going to be a carnival starting at 9 AM. The local Presbyterian church had been kind enough to pool its resources and throw an outdoor "kids day" complete with moonwalks, free food, balloons and live music. I saw a man with a baby and a little girl, so I stopped to give them the details. He told me that he was looking for someone who was supposed to meet them around that time. I thought he said they were coming from Tennessee.

Well, the next day I was walking through, praying, and I saw the same man and his two girls still there. I was a little confused, so I asked if he found who he was looking for. He pointed to another little girl that was with them and smiled, saying she was who they had been looking for. He told me he didn't need anything else, but

I already knew that from the look on his face. They were all going — together — to Las Vegas as soon as their ride came.

As we were talking, a Red Cross volunteer came up and talked to him. His fiancée had lost her anti-anxiety medicine and was having a hard time. I asked him if I could pray for his family. He told me his name was Gilbert. I just prayed for God to guide and protect them and that, if they didn't know Him, that He'd reach out and draw them to Himself.

Later on, I heard Gilbert's name announced, calling him to catch his ride to Las Vegas. They were on their way — with our prayers and love going with them.

We rejoiced in stories like these. We couldn't get the faces out of our minds once we left the shelter at night. People rushed up to us when they saw our Red Cross ID badges. Many had been wearing the same clothes for ten days, and it was obvious. They begged for shirts and pants or skirts, saying, "I'll wear anything! I'll wear anything, just please get me a something clean." It turns out many of the volunteers promised to find clothes, but simply disappeared into the crowd and didn't bring anything back.

We vowed that we would bring something back for the people. We crouched next to cots, looked into people's eyes and asked what each person needed. Many evacuees responded with, "You're the first person to ask me that." A hint of dignity was restored in those moments. All of a sudden, the evacuees were not among the missing in action, they were important individuals who mattered to us, and especially to God.

We would then run into the back of the convention center to the distribution room, which was actually only a concrete loading dock filled with boxes of clothes. We all did our best every day to sort the clothes into categories first thing in the morning. Then we would go through the clothes and fill orders. Each team member would look carefully through the donated items, trying to find the perfect shirt for a fifteen-year-old girl or a nice dress for an elderly lady. All stained and torn items (and there were many) were thrown away and not given out to the people. They deserved the best we could find.

The faces of our students brightened every time a gift was received with joy! They'd run back into the distribution center, chatting happily with each other about needing another skirt for Esther or finding some jeans that would fit Leroy. We all became good shoppers, excited that we could meet the physical needs of so many people.

Where is God when your world shatters? He is living through His children. He is making His way known to those who doubt. He is finding a towel with your initials on it. Just to bring you joy.

Our prayer for the team was this: "Lord, break our hearts with the things that break yours. Give us your heart of compassion." Our prayers were answered, as one by one the student's hearts opened and blossomed.

It started the minute we walked into the shelter and saw an elderly lady sitting in her wheelchair by her cot. Her hands covered her face as if she couldn't bear to look at the new world around her, as if she were completely lost. It continued in conversations every day...

PLACEMENT TAKES OFF

The placement service we are offering is beginning to take off. People are getting ready to leave but they also <u>didn't</u> want to leave. No one wanted to go because they all thought they'd be able to return to their homes right away. It is hard to explain that the city will not be open to return to for quite awhile. And, even when you can return, if your home was underwater, it's either gone or worthless. Hard to comprehend, isn't it. "Sorry, your house is gone." Where do houses go? Washed into the yards of those who also lost their homes.

This culture runs so deep that the people here do not travel. New generations of people live in the same homes their parents lived in. Your block is your world. The idea of relocating hours or days away to a new home is just unthinkable for many of them. I spoke with one woman today who had no clue where North Carolina was located.

Yet, a few are willing to go. They are desperate. They can't take the shelter any longer. The addicts are going nuts. They're desperate for drugs. The medication they need to help them through withdrawal seems to be unavailable. I wonder what host families would do if we sent them one of the addicts? That would really test anybody's generosity.

It's amazing to watch the team deal so quickly with the pain they experience during the day. They are unafraid to go back each day. In fact, they are asking for more time in the shelters. One volunteered to take the night shift at the River Center. We cry a lot and worship more. Somewhere in it all we are made whole so that we can go back and serve again the next day.

One AIM intern worked for a large part of two days on getting a large family into a home. AIM had over 1,000 families or individuals contact us after the hurricane, saying that they would be willing to take evacuees into their own homes and give them shelter. However, no one was willing to take in a family of six, four of whom were kids.

Our staff could see the look of desperation on the father's face. His name was Lionel. Just when she was about to give up, two things happened at once. First, a man and a woman we didn't know were walking the floors looking for a lost relative. They thought their relative had been killed in the storm and that they had been searching in vain the entire time.

Our staff and these relatives happened to bump into each other in the midst of the huge crowd. The AIM interns read the relatives' sign asking for (ready?) Lionel! It was the <u>same</u> Lionel! She had the great joy of telling this man and woman that Lionel and his family were still alive!

Then, someone returned a phone call to our Placement Desk about the family of six. It was a man who told us that he had three extra bedrooms. He was leaving for France that day and would be gone for three weeks. He was leaving his house key in his garage! Lionel's family was welcome to "come on home!"

Over and over, God showed the evacuees that He loves them and He cares about them as individuals. He gave them loving signs, small and large. Towels. Homes. Hope...

Ashley Seidlitz, AIM intern
Alberta, Canada

I asked to work at the placement table at the Istrouma Baptist Church center. I walked into the building and was blown away by the amount of people and the Military Police guarding the entrances to control the crowds.

I glanced to the right and there was our AIM table, where conversations would take place that would change my life. I didn't even think *about the things that God could do with me that day. I was only thinking about how I was unqualified to find homes for these people or to make them understand that there was a better place than a shelter to live. I was so afraid to try and bring hope to these people. After all, who am I? I'm just this girl from Canada, how could I make a difference?*

We reached the table; there were five of us girls, Elizabeth, Mandy, Emily, Camilla and myself. Phones in hand ready to go, I received my instructions: "Find a host family somewhere in the state closest to your family's needs."

They handed me a binder with around 600 host families and an atlas of the United States of America. "Sure, ask the Canadian *girl to do the American geography," was the thought that went through my mind.*

9:00 a.m. hit and we started to work. A guy sat down to talk to me. I was so nervous about not being able to help, but I asked him all the standard procedure questions. He was 27 years old, African-American and had lost everything. He just wanted to get away and start over. "I want to go to Vancouver, Canada," he said.

I was astonished; he didn't even know that I had grown up in Alberta. We started talking about Canada, traveling, his dreams, what he does for work. His name was Cornelio; he just wanted to get away, travel, build a new life. I told him that I would look into Northern contacts but was pretty sure there weren't any in Canada yet.

He left and I got to work. The noise of the rushing people, kids running, and everyone else who was also looking for new homes was shut out. After about a half-hour of searching, a place jumped out at me. A 900 sq. ft. guesthouse, transportation, and "as long as needed" was in the comment box. Maybe, just maybe, this would work. So, I called the number.

A lady by the name of Christine answered the phone. I relayed the situation to her; right away she said, "Yes, that could definitely work." I relayed the information to Cornelio. I told him I found him a place — his own place in Connecticut. He said that was fine; he just wanted <u>out</u>. He blew me away that he would go and do anything just to get "out."

I then arranged a telephone meeting for Cornelio and his host family. I didn't get to hear the conversation between Cornelio and Christine, but afterward he sought me out. With tears in his eyes he said, "I have a home, they are supplying me with my own house, my own vehicle. Christine found me a job! The community wants to shower me with blessings and help me get back on my feet. Thank you!"

It was so amazing. God showed me that he uses the

weak, the clueless, and the inexperienced to do mighty
things. He allowed me to help be Hope to the
Hopelessness and give someone a new start.

Day Two was ending. Lives were changing before our
eyes. Our own lives too. God puts us in the position to
give, and then demonstrates the truth that, "It is better
to give than to receive."

Bethany Marron, AIM intern
Rhode Island

Inside the shelters I saw children running around with
absolutely no supervision, and elderly people shifting
uncomfortably, confined to their cots. Though it was clear
that the basic needs of these people were being taken
care of, there was a lingering sense of despair. Each army
cot represented both a story of survival and some tale of
tragedy. It was unreal to me. When I left the shelter after
the first day, I was probably more confused than when I
had entered. Despite all I had seen and the few stories I
had heard, there was something still missing. An unan-
swered, lingering tragedy.

The obvious answer to my question came on Day Two
from a pastor's wife. Her name was Sandy Brown. It was
late in the afternoon when a fellow AIM intern and I were
approached by a leader and asked to baby-sit Mrs. Brown's
three children.

The leader explained that the family had been dis-
placed from New Orleans and they were living with friends
in Louisiana. They needed the opportunity to enter the
shelter and register with the Red Cross. After a very hot
hour-and-a half outside the River Center, Mrs. Brown re-
emerged from the shelter and proceeded to express her
gratitude for our time.

We began to ask the "polite' questions about how she and her family had weathered the storm. It was her response that touched me. She began to share all that her family had lost, their home and worldly possessions, the comfort and security her children had felt in their school and local neighborhood. She proceeded to share her family's sorrow over losing their ministry; the children and families they had invested in and taken care of were gone and what was worse, she did not know their fate.

Finally, she stated, very poignantly, that she had no idea how anyone who endured Katrina would truly survive without Christ. It was clear that this seasoned Christian family was clinging to Christ and His promises during this unspeakable trial. As we prayed with Mrs. Brown and her family, I choked up in shame, realizing the lack of urgency I had placed on the gospel. It was clear to the Brown family and now to me how each person in the River Center was in desperate need of the saving knowledge of Christ.

I am thankful for Sandy Brown and her family, as God used their testimony in my life to challenge and encourage an elemental principal in Christianity...without Christ there is NO hope.

TOO GOOD TO BE TRUE?

<u>Stefanie Brunson, AIM intern</u>
<u>Alabama</u>

On the second day in the shelter, our team was supposed to walk around after lunch and ask the Lord what He wanted us to do. I decided I would go to the back room of the shelter because there had not been many volunteers back there. As I was walking around, I passed a man in a wheelchair. I felt the Lord say to go talk to him. As I approached him, I asked him if I could get anything for him. He said he didn't need anything, so I sat down and started talking.

He told me his story about how he got out of New Orleans and all of the things he had to overcome. His house was filled with a few inches of water — and about 20 minutes later it was filled with <u>eight</u> feet of water. He said that he and his brother lost everything. Their names are Glenn and Rosairo.

He said as they were trying to get out, people were passing in boats and refusing to help. Glenn said that he and his brother finally got on a bus, but they had to pay $5 each. Glenn and Rosairo both suffered from a lot of health problems, so that just made it even more difficult to leave. Glenn said he had to leave his two dogs because they were not allowed to take them. After I finished talking with him, I asked if I could pray with him and he seemed more than happy to let me.

That night after we left the shelter I could not stop thinking about Glenn. I prayed for him a lot that night. My parents own some apartments back home in AL. I thought I could ask them if we had a vacant one and if two men from New Orleans could stay there rent-free. I was so excited that night before I went to bed. The next day I called home and my mom said she didn't think there were any open apartments. My dad called later that day and said that they would have a vacancy and it would be fine if they stayed rent-free.

I went back to Glenn and Rosairo and told them the good news. They were very appreciative, but a little skeptical because they didn't know my parents. Rosairo decided he wanted to talk to my dad first before he decided anything. After he talked to my dad, he seemed much more excited and confident about the whole situation. After he got off the phone, he came back to Glenn and said, "Well, it looks like we are moving to Alabama." I was so excited for them. He said that he didn't want to make his final decision so fast, so he was going to call my parents in the next two days. I don't exactly know the final decision but hopefully I'll find out tomorrow.

It was as if it was all "too good to be true." For once, something that sounded too good to be true wasn't after all.

A MIRACULOUS PLACEMENT STORY

Janae Martin, AIM intern
Pennsylvania

One situation where God really amazed me was the placement of an Indian family in Houston, Texas. I met this soon-to-be mother while she was waiting in a distribution line. She was nervous about the birth of her child because her doctor had told her that her present living conditions were dangerous for her baby. I asked her if I could pray with her. She smiled gratefully and held my hand tight.

After the prayer, I told her I would attempt to find her (and her family) a home before the birth of her child. But I told her it would be difficult because her family had **10** members.

Well, I went to the placement center and one of the girls pointed out to me that there was an Indian family in Texas that wanted to provide a home for Indian evacuees!

I called the man in Texas and let him talk to the head of this Indian household. They talked for awhile and after they hung up, the man was smiling. He grinned at me and said, "I know this man, he is a distant relation! We found him now and we will go live with them!"

I was completely amazed at the power and grace of God. He took a completely tragic situation and used it to reunite a family!

Janeen's Journal:

Cesar and Jennifer called later that day. They found Tyanka! Tyanka also found her other son at the Astrodome! Two more miracles! All of them went to Corpus Christi. Cesar and Jennifer were able to get them set up with the medical attention her mom needed, and the shelter that would help them get into an apartment. I also was able to speak to Tyanka for a little while. It was great news. God had mercy on us again.

That morning I met an elderly woman named Doris. She said that she had no one left and she would go any-where. By this time, I had been dialoguing quite a bit with a contact in Wilmington, NC.

The people there had the best thing going for evac-uees who wanted to start over somewhere new, with the possible exception of a NEW storm, Hurricane Ophelia, approaching the area. Her volunteer center had everything an evacuee could want or need from a new place to go, food, apartments and homes, furniture, gift certificates, medical aid, schooling, job opportunities, etc.

Doris thought that all of that sounded good, and she was ready to go. We set her up with a bus ticket and got her to the Greyhound station. We gave her our phone numbers, the number of the woman in Wilmington, and information on where she was going. Then, I gave her a sign to hold once she arrived. Off she went from uncer-tainty into the unknown.

At the end of the day, Ben exhorted the group to consider, at a new level, what it means to lay down our personal rights. As humans, but especially as Americans, we believe we have a right to things such as privacy, fairness, our own bedroom, 24-hour freedom, and so on. So many in the world do not have the rights we have. To serve these people, or simply to be radical in following God, we must be willing to allow our rights to be stripped from us.

This includes our rights to comfort, to chose our future direction and even to life. As someone said recently, "Obedience is not a personal choice, it is a calling." For there to be great success, there must always be great sacrifice.

The Spirit of God landed on us in power. The response in worship and surrender was absolutely incredible. How could we control our lives when we saw how effectively we were able to minister once we laid down control and rights? It was a sweet night.

<u>Jenny Barton, AIM intern</u>
<u>Texas</u>

My first few days at River Center in Baton Rouge always ended in the realization that I hadn't talked to any evacuees. It is always so hard for me to overcome being shy, so I seem to end up working "behind the scenes." I started working on Sunday by serving grits to the residents of the arena.

I prayed that God could use me to talk to others. Then, after a debriefing with my team, I went up to the infirmary to help out. After what had seemed to be "down time," a woman walked into the infirmary after talking to FEMA, with a girl from our group. To tell you the truth, she scared me! She was very outspoken and had a dry humor that I didn't relate to very well. After serving lunch and picking up trash, something drew me over to her.

My teammates Robby and Deanna were talking to her about how to "doctor" her hangnail. I walked up and just listened to the conversation. Soon I found myself just asking her questions about her life. Her eyes just lit up as she went back into time to tell us of her history.

She shared about her travels and gave me advice, while I just sat on a cooler and just soaked it all in. She reminded me of my great-grandfather and his wonderful stories. That was something that took us both into our own happy memories. She also spoke of being a prominent journalist in New York.

After having to leave our long conversation, I realized that God had sent a conversation to me that was so much more than I expected!

So many of our conversations were like that. We felt awkward starting out, but as we began talking, we were drawn in, and in the end didn't want to leave.

September 11, 2005

"BRIGHT LIGHTS 24/7"

If you've ever had a truly inconsiderate neighbor, you know how they can disrupt your life. Think about people playing acid-rock at 4 a.m. with a thump that's reminiscent of a heartbeat from hell; the guy with the motorcycle that's so loud car alarms go off as he passes by; or, the dysfunctional screams of families locked in marital combat. All you want is for the noise to stop.

Now, roll up all the sleepless nights your neighbors may have caused you and multiply that din and aggravation by four or five thousand and you've got a picture of what it was like to sleep at one of the shelters. Shelters filled with bedraggled, discouraged, tired and angry people. Bright lights 24/7. Odors. Moans and movement all day and night, every day and night. And all you want is for it to stop.

The wise fled before the storm. The cautious stayed away afterward. Those now living in the shelter wonder if those that stayed were better off than the primal conditions of the shelter.

Alli Mellon:

Baton Rouge, a city transformed from 300,000 people to 800,000 people in the past eleven days, is a shelter for the now-homeless, a refuge for those driven from their homes by violent wind and waves. We've seen it on the television and headlining the papers. We've all watched the water rise in New Orleans and seen the coast of Mississippi swallowed up.

But now that I am here, seeing it all with my own eyes, it's different. Within seconds of arriving I had tears in my eyes, the first of many times I would cry with the people, especially with those at the River Center.

So far, AIM has placed over seventy evacuees with families who contacted us and were willing to take them in. We could write volumes and never record all of the stories we've heard in 15 hours with these evacuees. I know that we will never forget the voices that told them.

In my head, I'll still hear the voice of the little girl who ran up to me, after seeing my badge, shouting, "Did you find my sister? Did you find my sister?"

Our students will never forget the words that God spoke in their ears as they just sat and listened and loved on people. The Lord put words of hope into the students' mouths and let it flow out onto the hopeless. Though as Christians we've known it in our hearts all along, we now see with our eyes that Jesus Christ is truly the only answer. He's the only hope. He's the only way out of a gym floor crowded with cots and guarded by military men with huge, black guns. He is the way.

May God give strength to the people who are coordinating our hurricane relief efforts and trying to place people in over 700 welcoming homes. With roots deep in New Orleans and the surrounding areas, it is hard for people to even consider relocating to another city.

So much work was being carried out by young people whom many older Christians might think are only interested in video games, cars that look like Matchbox toys, tattoos or the latest fashions. But here they were. Sinking their hearts and souls into the lives of strangers. The exhausted serving the exhausted.

SAME DAY; DIFFERENT SHELTER

Istrouma Baptist is a thriving church located just of I-12 East. The church quickly cleared space in their old building to be used for a shelter. In a matter of hours there were 700 people living there. The entire church staff suddenly became a staff of one of the largest shelters in Baton Rouge. They were up for the task.

The church allowed a group of the AIM intern volunteers to work in both the shelter and a distribution center set up by the church. Donations were pouring from all over the country and they desperately needed help sorting through them so the donations could be given out in an orderly and efficient way.

At times the amount of donations pouring into the distribution center made order and efficiency impossible. Churches would send a semi-truck load of food or clothing without sorting it or boxing it and just dump it on the doorstep of Istrouma and expect the already over worked staff to deal with it with thankful hearts!

This is part of the reason why the AIM intern team was so valuable to this shelter. They modeled true service and worked hard. At times the team was able to pause from work and play with the kids as well though.

Josh Plett, AIM intern
Manitoba, Canada

One day I was able to play "'kickball" with a group of young children at the Istrouma Baptist Church.

Justin O'Hara, my teammate, and I played this game the kids made up. It's like baseball except instead of using a baseball they used a soccer ball. To see the joy on these kids' faces amidst all the pain surrounding them. People sweating and kids crying. Just the pain and fear on people's faces, really hit me hard. I've never seen anything like it.

We played for maybe 20 or 30 minutes, but after we were done the thrill on a boy named Jevaunte's face really touched me. He came running up to me and jumped into my arms and squeezed. He said, "Thank you sir for playing with me." To hear him say that, with the meaning behind it really touched me and brought tears to my eyes. To let him go and see him run back to his parents back at the church gym was tough because he said he didn't know what would happen next. I ask that all of you just keep these kids in your thoughts and prayers. They don't know what's next. The older I get I know that no one really knows what's next, but it's harder on kids sometimes.

<u>Danielle Kloepper, another AIM intern from Texas, was able to connect with kids in a different way. This is a story from her journal:</u>

The first time I walked into the gym where the people slept, I recall feeling one thing – darkness. Not just the darkness you see, but the kind you feel. Row after row of cots with old and young alike. Most babies had no cribs; they slept next to their mothers. Being a kid lover, I could hardly hold back from going toward the children.

One family will forever be held close to my heart. I was unsure of how to approach them because their mother seemed so sad that she was angry. I didn't have to do much because Carleto, the oldest boy, came running up to me followed by the youngest girl, about 2, Alysia. The first day was spent coloring, playing with balls and Carleto's personal favorite, the merry-go-round.

I remember the way it felt to go from inside to outside — the contrast of light and darkness made you feel better. You could look into their eyes and see the hope and innocence, the confusion and the peace only a child can hold.

The next morning when I walked into the gym and looked toward Carleto's cot, I saw his little sister in tears and Carleto curled up in a ball. He was sick. Their mother was nowhere to be seen so, without thought, I picked up the baby. She was coughing and as she held me close, I felt her feverish skin. Her eye was swollen shut with green goo coming out.

All I could do was hold her until her Mom returned. I was soon called away to another task and didn't see the

kids until the next day, when their grandfather
approached me outside. "Thank you," he said, "my
daughter is tired and you have no idea what an extra
hand means." We continued to talk and I was able to
pray with him.

Carleto ran out to greet me. With the humor of a
young boy, he told me that his grandpa brought him to
the doctor and "they stuck something up my butt and it
melted." Being a nursing major, I could only laugh and
thank God for healing his body.

SAME DAY, YET ANOTHER SHELTER

The Livingston Community Center became a shelter by default. Two other shelters that were located in schools nearby had to close down once classes resumed. The evacuees needed a place to live, so The Livingston Community Center was chosen. The Red Cross staff here was small but very organized. They quickly saw the potential in our AIM intern volunteers and plugged them into jobs.

We quickly learned the shelter was very small and so the kids needed outdoor activities. There was no shade to protect them from the sun. We decided to bring the army tent from our campsite at the church over to be used as shade for the kids.

<u>Christy Rios, an AIM intern from California, gives insight to first reactions of our team at LCC in her journal:</u>

As we arrived at Livingston Community Center in
Baton Rouge, my eyes were captivated by what I saw. The
shelter was in total chaos. Barefoot children wandering
around crying. Fathers and mothers lying down in dis-
tress.

I continued my journey through the shelter into the
infirmary. As I entered, my heart broke into tears. Men
and women of all ages suffering from numerous sickness-

es. I began to offer my assistance wherever needed. From changing wet bed linens, to sweeping, to praying, to smiling, to just being like Jesus. As I was changing a bed linen, my ears were drawn to the cry of a little boy.

I hurried to him and asked his grandmother why he was in tears. She helplessly looked at me and said, "He wants to go outside."

"I don't blame him," said some others who were bound to their so-called beds. I asked the little boy if I could take him outside. His tears immediately dried up and he excitedly nodded yes. I lifted him into my arms and held him close to my heart.

We left the smell of urine, the smell of pain and the smell of depression and took in a glorious breath of God's beautiful creation. The little boy began to play, filled with laughter and smiles. He ran, jumped and enjoyed some time on the swings. My heart was forever changed. I smiled at that moment and I thanked God for that opportunity to bring joy and love to a child who was in desperate need.

Did I bring Jesus to that child? Or, the child to Jesus?

A SAD ANNIVERSARY AND A VIRUS

Today is the fourth anniversary of the World Trade Center attacks. We visited churches today where our team has been serving. For many of us it's been the best week of ministry and yet the most challenging week of ministry ever.

Six people on our team are now infected with a virus from the shelters. They are very sick. We are isolating them and pushing the others to get the rest they need, and to minimize close contact with evacuees in the shelter for the last day. The virus, once medicated, takes 24 hours to clear from the body. We hope they are ready for the drive home on Tuesday — to begin their originally scheduled mission trips.

Janeen's Journal:

Ben and I were still unsure of how long we would stay in Baton Rouge. By this time, we were so tired that we were afraid to sleep because we thought we might never get up. We started to think about returning with the team on Tuesday.

Ben and Janeen went to church at River Community and afterward visited Istrouma Baptist Church, where some of our crew were serving. The operation there was calm, organized, and peaceful compared to the River Center.

Our contact in Wilmington, NC called and said that Doris — the lady who evacuated there the other day — did not arrive when she was supposed to. We assumed that she may have gotten confused at one of the connections she had to make, and we trusted that someone was kind enough to redirect her.

In the evening, we planned on doing a worship service for some of the military who requested it, but when we got there no one showed up. The guys who planned on coming had a last-minute order to go to LSU. We ended up sitting in the hallway and spending some time in prayer and worship. One of the evacuees joined us midway through. It felt good to be able to pray with people inside the shelter, where all of our other time was dominated by needs that we could not meet most of the time.

God knew we needed to go there that night to have a simple, yet powerful encounter with Him for ourselves. We went to give care and love to others, and God cared for us instead.

LONELINESS

One of the loneliest places in the world can be a crowd full of strangers, where you feel totally alone and disconnected. But Jesus understands loneliness and estrangement and sorrow, and He never leaves nor forsakes His children. A AIM intern summed it up well.

Andrea Kreller, AIM intern
Washington

I saw Kenneth just sitting by himself under the shade at a picnic table far from everyone. I walked up to him, asked how he was, introduced myself, and asked if I could join him. Kenneth, like many people, had lost his home in floods. He was at the shelter with his daughter, son-in-law and grandchildren. This was actually the third home he had lost due to natural disasters, so he was no stranger to such things. He and his family had many decisions to make. Should they wait to go home and rebuild or start anew?

It is so hard to leave your home, the place where you grew up; can you even imagine being forced to do this? What truly amazed me about this man is that even though he had suffered so much, most of his sorrow was for others. He saw the brokenness all around him, the unknown, the confusion, the anger, the disbelief, broken promises from the authorities, and all the things that go along with the situation.

It was as if he took it all and put it upon his shoulders. What a truly selfless attitude! I remember watching his eyes grow misty, trying to fight the tears that wouldn't stop coming. I had the wonderful opportunity to pray for this man and share the hope of the Lord with him. He was so grateful and we were both truly blessed by our conversation. It was hard for me to leave but I did, knowing that the Lord is with him and his family. He is in awesome hands.

September 12, 2005

FINAL DAY ON THE FRONT LINES FOR THE AIM INTERNS

We had now been on-site for four days. The work thus far was grueling. Not "stuck in traffic for four hours" grueling...this was non-stop, sleep on the floor, eat what you can, when you can, flat-out grueling. But we knew when our trials would be over. For the thousands of unfortunate folks we were helping, it wasn't going to end anytime soon. Maybe not for years.

Here's how one person put it...

> Katie Oswald, AIM intern
> New Jersey
>
> *There was never a lack of things to do at the River Center. I was fully immersed in the efforts. I had heard a few people's stories and had asked God to break my heart for these people. It was not until the fourth day that He blatantly answered my prayer.*
>
> *It was noon and I had the job of pumping hand sanitizer into the hands of everyone who was in line for lunch. The line was already at least 100 yards long, but I paused at about the 20th person because lunch was running late.*
>
> *Celebrities were addressing the crowd. I stood uneasily among three men who were mocking the fact that famous people were at the shelter paying a visit. I became embarrassed for the celebrities, as I wondered if they knew these people weren't interested in what they had to say and whether or not the celeb's really "loved them." All the people wanted were some honest answers and tools to get back into the world. And they wanted lunch. They were hungry.*

One of the men then decided to take a seat a few feet away from where I was standing. I saw an empty chair near him and my mind immediately raced. "Should I sit down?" "How could I ever possibly relate to this guy — I'm a White teenage girl whose house was still standing?" "How could I share Jesus' love to this guy?"

A few seconds later, I heard myself asking if I could sit down, bracing myself for some awkward silence. I need not have feared, not only did Will allow me to sit with him, he started the conversation.

Will helped me get a glimpse of what the survivors had gone through and were continuing to go through. At first, I shrugged off his repetitive statement, "This is a critical situation." Then he made it personal.

"Katie," he said, "what would you do if someone called you up and said your house in New Jersey was 14 feet under water? That no one knew where your mom and dad were and that your neighbors were seen floating, dead." Usually priding myself in my ability to hide my emotions, I was surprised when I could not stop the tears from escaping.

Will continued to share with me. He was pretty discouraged about things going on, and skeptical of those who had been helping in the relief efforts. I did my best to assure him that most were pouring their hearts into the efforts and it was genuine. He shared with me that his wife had left him immediately after the disaster and how much it hurt him. He said when the day comes that I am married, that my husband and I become one and to stick with my man, no matter what.

Looking back on that conversation, I praise God for answering my prayer to really have had the chance to share some of the pain with all the people there. I also praise God for, despite obvious differences, allowing me to form a short bond with Will. Maybe there was no in-depth talk, but I know Will knows there is a God, and I will be praying for God to move in his life.

100 TO 1

There were so many "Wills" who needed what we offered. We figured there were 100 evacuees for every one of us. In our smallness, God was Big...

Kelsey Manfredi, AIM intern
Virginia

Over the next few days, I was allowed to serve the multitudes. I sanitized their hands to keep disease from spreading, I brought them their meals, and I helped them find new clothes to replace those they had lost. Yet, the best service I was able to provide to them was my ability to listen to their stories and offer the comfort of Christ.

During the four days I spent at the River Center, I was able to have many specific conversations about the hope of Christ with the unbelieving evacuees. Yet, I proudly entered the River Center confident that I was the one who would be the vessel of change. As always – God shattered my assumptions. Apart from Him we can do nothing, but through Him we can do "all things." It's not what we do for God; it's what He does through us that changes eternity.

SHORT ON TIME

As our time was running out and our energy as well, we found refreshment from those we served...

Alli Mellon:

Today I met Mrs. A. She sat in a wheelchair on the

edge of the crowd, a baby blanket draped over her shoulders and a smile on her face. When I knelt down to talk to her, she immediately began praising the Lord. She told me over and over, "these people have nothing to complain about. You all have been so nice to us! Some of them here have more clothes now than they did before! Praise the Lord that He spared us!"

She continued to encourage me, listing all of the things she was thankful for. I had been talking with her for a long while when she finally told me that one of her sons was still missing. She was heartbroken about this, and praying that he would show up, but continued to praise God for the family that He had spared, the ones he had given her.

She was a light in a dark place. She told me as she looked around at the crowd, "I don't know how they do this without hope. I don't know how they do this without Jesus."

"Come to me, all you who are weary and burdened, and I will give you rest," (Matt. 11:28).

DORIS IS FOUND!

We finally were able to locate Doris, the evacuee we had placed in North Carolina.

Janeen's Journal:

It was my sixth consecutive day at the shelter. Fewer people were inquiring about housing opportunities. Some were having breakdowns. They needed to get out but did not know how. FEMA could not provide all the answers people expected of them. Words cannot describe our feelings of stress and inadequacy.

That afternoon I was getting very worried about Doris.

I called Missing Persons and they were very helpful. The man on the phone found out where she made her connections. He called back later to say that she made it to Wilmington and was with the woman who was looking for her. Praise God! I found out later that Doris has a mild case of Alzheimer's and I think she was just a little lost for a while. She is now living with a roommate in an assisted-living condominium.

I spent a couple of hours with a young woman named Stefanie. She wanted to leave the shelter but didn't want to go until she found her dad. He was driving a bus for the city the day that Katrina came, and she had no information on how to contact him. We spent a while trying to figure out ways to get in touch with him, but we came up with nothing.

The air conditioning in the shelter was icy cold every day and she was shivering so badly that Ben went and found her a long sleeved shirt. I wanted to be able to help her more than I did, but she was intent on finding her father. After she left, I never saw her again.

THE FINAL NIGHT

Alli Mellon recalls the last hours of the four-day mission to Louisiana in her journal:

Our final night in Baton Rouge arrived. We were a group of broken people. We were sharing stories with each other.

Jason from the Mexico team told about his long days of working in the shelter infirmary. He had been taking care of a little boy with autism. The boy lay in his bed, ignored by his mother, soaked in his own urine. The mother would disappear for two hours at a time. But, if *anyone in the infirmary tried to care for the boy or change his diaper, she would fly into a rage and curse at them, demanding that they get away from her son.*

But Jason was different. Jason got through to her. Somehow, he was able to reach this woman who was so angry, so bitter, so desperate. They connected over the bed of a little boy in a makeshift hospital.

As Jason told us his story, he began to realize that tomorrow no one would be there to take his place with that family. He wouldn't be there to love that child, to take care of him, to play with him, and the mother would not let another person do it. He began to weep, to openly sob, and to grieve for that family. It wrecked all of us and our tears began.

The AIM interns were young. They were untrained. Most of them were inexperienced in grief that cut this deep. But we brought them to Baton Rouge with a lot of hope to offer. As we watched these students hugging babies, helping mothers, taking the arms of old men who slowly made their way down the long aisles, we saw the love of Christ. We saw relationship. We saw a fire in their hearts to go home and motivate their friends, families and churches to "Come to Baton Rouge!" We saw them change...and broken.

We felt like Peter and John must have felt in Acts 4: "Now when they saw the boldness of Peter and John, and perceived that they were unlearned and ignorant men, they marveled; and they took knowledge of them, that they had been with Jesus.?" (Acts 4:13)

"WE HAD BEEN WITH JESUS"

We didn't come to Louisiana with simple answers to life's most difficult puzzles. We were "unlearned." The Greek word would apply today to someone without a college degree, for example. And, we probably appeared as "ignorant" to some. The Greek root here is even more graphic; we get our English word "idiot" from it. But, none of that mattered. The people around us marveled at what God was doing through us, and they knew "we had been with Jesus."

Katie Riedberger, AIM intern
Michigan

One particular girl, whose name was Lamani, became so precious to me, despite my efforts not to get too emotionally attached. Her sweet face and little hands captured my heart. I called her "My Cuddlebug."

Throughout the four days we were there we spent our time ministering to the kids, trying to keep them occupied and give their parents a break, I was able to form a bond with her. She seemed desperate for love and attention.

So many of the kids already come from homes where the parents don't give them enough attention. After going through a traumatic experience such as they did — there was almost desperation in Lamani's hugs as she clung to me on our last day. As I left the shelter I said good-bye...but with the knowledge that she is indeed in the Lord's hands, as I had prayed.

It was as if Jesus in a brown AIM shirt showed up and handed out Bread to every person, even when there was not enough bread to go around. It was as if Jesus were there in the breakfast and lunch lines, serving up eggs and singing praise songs in the midst of Scientology volunteers, atheists, and soldiers. He showed up in the middle of kick-ball games and handicap meals...

Beth Arnold, AIM intern
Pennsylvania

Going to Baton Rouge I expected a lot of things, homeless and sick people, destroyed houses and trees. I came into each center expecting people to be angry and tired, depressed and all alone.

To my utter amazement, each day in the midst of all the exhausted confusion was someone full of gratitude and hope. On my last day, while serving at a church distribution center, I had the supreme pleasure of serving such a woman.

JoAnn, the first lady I helped that day had a newborn baby, and absolutely nothing else. Until that day, she hadn't been able to get any help. She and a friend had found each other and were struggling to survive. For the better part of an hour, I dug through clothing and shoe bins, baby blankets, toiletries and baby bottles. Carrying three garbage bags and two arm-fulls I returned to her, victorious from my hunt!

As I presented to her item after item her eyes filled with tears, and she kept crying out, "Thank you, Baby, you've done such a good job, you don't know what this means to us."

I know I didn't save the world that day, but I know that I made hers a little more worth living in. That was so cool. God is so great!

It was if Jesus were digging though dusty boxes of clothes for that perfect pair of pants or that unstained baby outfit. It was Jesus who put His words of hope into the students' mouths. Jesus shone in the eyes of the AIM interns who begged not to go home that last morning, to let them go and check on Ann one more time or serve just one more breakfast to Merlin.

He was there. We felt Him. We saw Him. And so did the people in shelters in Baton Rouge.

"JUST ASK THE BROWN T-SHIRT PEOPLE"
We didn't go for the praise of man, but God gave us favor with

other shelter volunteers, the military and the Red Cross. Our AIM interns received many kind words from those who watched them serve. Whenever the National Guard or Red Cross were too overwhelmed to respond to an evacuee they would say, "Just ask the brown t-shirt people." The brown AIM shirt was our uniform, but we believe it was Jesus they saw in us.

One Red Cross director stopped Ben Messner on his way out of the River Center shelter and pleaded with him to not take the group of brown t-shirt people away. He said, "We don't know what we will do with out them here."

Even though this praise was nice, it was often what the children said that meant the most.

<u>Amanda Wyatt, AIM intern</u>
<u>Michigan</u>

During my time at the River Center, there were many people who really affected my life, but one girl really stands out. I met Arianna while walking up one of the long rows of beds. I was just talking to some of the little kids that were just playing everywhere — on beds, in aisles, everywhere you looked.

Arianna was about eight years-old and so adorable. She was a chubby little girl with lots of long braids in her hair and the sweetest face. We got some kids' books to read together, but she was more interested in talking and asking questions. She was sitting on a blue and red mat and she asked me to sit down with her. After reading and talking some, she started to work on a book with lots of puzzles in it and I helped her with that.

I was glad I got to help her do things to help stimulate learning because so many of these kids' parents just didn't have time or energy to spend any quality time with their kids — and many kids didn't even have their parents with them.

She kept asking to play "duck, duck, goose" so we started a game with another girl from my team and another little girl from the shelter. We played for about 15 minutes. Before we were finished, a little boy in a bed nearby joined us, along with a few more of my team members and another staff guy we didn't know. It was really good to see these kids playing together because a lot of them didn't interact unless there was a big game or something they could join in.

When I got up to leave, she came over and gave me a hug and said in a sweet, quiet voice, "I'll miss you."

It was so hard to leave her and all of the kids there. They connected to people who gave them attention really fast and really didn't want their new friends to leave. It was hard to explain to Arianna that I had to leave and wasn't coming back.

She definitely affected me with a sweet, peaceful spirit. I will never forget her. I'll miss her, too. For the rest of my life.

THE LORD WILL SEND LABORERS

<u>Andrea Kreller, AIM intern</u>
<u>Washington</u>

While I was serving in Baton Rouge, there were many ministry opportunities. My personal favorite opportunity was simply talking to the people who had been through the disaster. They appreciated our just being a listening ear and allowing them to share their stories, what they lost, how they got out and what their future plans were.

But the best part was praying with them and sharing the hope of the Lord. Their eyes often just filled with tears. The people are aching for love, personal attention and hope. So many of them feel lost. And they have lost everything.

The Lord just broke my heart for these people and I'm thankful for the opportunity to build relationships with them.

They will be in my prayers. I left with the confidence that the Lord is still there and will send more volunteers.

September 13, 2005

A CALL FOR REINFORCEMENTS

Seth Barnes:

I write to you with a full heart from Baton Rouge. The days of serving in the midst of this disaster relief effort have humbled me.

AIM's response to the Hurricane deal was initially to develop a placement service for evacuees to relocate into a host family apartment or home. We also sent the AIM intern teams to minister to evacuees on the ground. I can report that the ministry of the AIM intern teams has been incredible. The military and the Red Cross and the churches that have shelters where we work have been singing our praises.

The placement service has really gone well. The man-hours it takes to get a family relocated are intense and overwhelming but we have placed over 100 people now. AIM has created a healthy reputation for being in the "relief business."

AIM responded early to the Hurricane Katrina crisis by setting up an online database for host families around the USA to sign up to receive an evacuee family or individual. The beginnings of the idea sound very romantic and many thought it would be a quick process. Yet, the exact opposite has proven to be true.

Here's what we have learned in this process of placing families:

1. New Orleans residents love, and do not want to leave, their beloved home. *The pride and culture in these people is both inspiring and challenging.*

2. Those willing to host evacuees thought the

evacuees would be jumping for opportunities to come live with them, and many applied strong pressure to speed the process along. *There was almost an attitude of arrogance on the part of some of the hosts. Others are incredibly patient and willing to serve evacuees in ways other than opening a home.*

3. Those from the South really want to stay in the South. *The vast majority are not interested in moving to Michigan, Utah, South Dakota, or Pennsylvania.*

4. The evacuees are in shock. *Thinking of making a major relocation into a person's home they do not know is more than are ready to handle so quickly.*

5. Building relationships is a key factor. *At times, buses would pull up to a shelter and shout, "Anyone who wants to go to [this place] there is a bus leaving in 45 minutes...who wants to go?"*

Sometimes these buses pulled away empty and other times they pulled away nearly full. It usually depended upon how many desperate people just were sitting around when the announcement was made or how bad the day had gone for the shelter. If it was a bad day, many would just say, "The heck with it. I am out of here." The buses had no screening process. The addicts and street people usually took these opportunities to relocate as well.

6. It's taken many, many hours to connect those who have actually been placed, but the reward has been incredible. *Usually both the family and the person or group placing the evacuees are in tears at departure. It's bittersweet but it's progress.*

7. Evacuees are very hesitant to leave before having their ID replaced. *Then there's the ordeal of getting FEMA checks, Social Security checks or other public services that are offered to them all settled. Many* *displaced people will not leave until they are sure their house is actually lost. Still others will not leave until they find their missing loved ones. Loyalty supersedes expediency and comfort. They are not going to just go away and leave their families — without knowing if they're dead or alive — behind.*

8. Many evacuees know a friend or relative (sometimes a very distant relative) in another place and they just need transportation to get there. *Placement service is often more about transportation service.*

Nevertheless, the reward is incredible once a family is placed. One placement saved a woman's life. Another placement will likely give the health necessary for two premature babies to survive. I do not think it an over-statement to say that those working in placement have made lasting friendships with those they have helped.

Last night and early this morning, the AIM intern team and Placement Service team quickly drove back to Atlanta in order to go to the far ends of the earth on their previously scheduled missions trips! Their time here wasn't even the mission trip they expected — it was simply a prologue!

It is humbling to see hearts so dedicated to the Lord's service and so willing to do the "dirty work" of Christian service. They were called to wipe noses and bottoms, care for the needy and the angry, serve and serve with little sleep, and give loving, godly care to those who believed no one cared. And it was all done in the name and by the Spirit of God.

There's a void right now in Louisiana. It's not that AIM's teams cannot be replaced. God has millions of people He can use to minister to the brokenhearted and hurting. You included.

This story doesn't end with our departure. It can end with having you join with others, to get involved. There are five pages that we have intentionally left blank at the end this book.

Even as we were writing our accounts of Hurricane Katrina, Hurricane Rita pounded the same region again, and devastated additional towns in Texas, as well. One thing's for sure. There will be no lack of opportunities to minister to others.

Janeen's Journal:

After that week—with all the people I met and things I saw, I will forever know and believe that the Katrina evacuees are true survivors. It was an honor to help in any way I was able, even if some days I only ended up being a sounding board for someone who was angry at the Red Cross. To listen and to acknowledge, to respond when a response was wanted...this was what a lot of it boiled down to. The crazy thing is that I liked it.

I was content being about the Lord's business and helping in any way that I could. The truth is it wasn't me, it was the Lord doing it all. He's our shelter in the midst of life's storms.

September 14, 2005

A CHALLENGE TO CONSIDER

The whole crew is back in Georgia now. The AIM intern team is healthy and tomorrow they all board flights for their different locations. We're confident they are ready to go and serve. They stretched themselves every day and were a true blessing to hundreds of relief workers and evacuees. The decision to relocate the training camp to Baton Rouge was the right one.

People were impressed by our work. Our response allowed AIM to continue recruiting for the relief effort. This is the worst storm ever to hit the coast of the untouchable United States. But there will be other storms.

This is the greatest opportunity for the Church to reach out in activist compassion since the Civil Rights movement. It is quite likely the opportunity of a lifetime. A whole city has been destroyed and is waiting to be rebuilt. How will we respond? How will you respond?

"God's will" isn't some inexplicable mystery. We arrived in Baton Rouge with so many questions, but as we began to serve Him, He opened the doors and "filled in the blanks."

Show Him you are willing. He will give you opportunities and the strength to change the world. One shelter at a time.

> Ben wrote this.
>
> *Every night since leaving Baton Rouge my dreams have taken me back to the shelters. I cannot get people out of my mind that are still there. I know I needed to leave and bring the team back to GA but I left my heart behind.*
>
> *Thank you Lord for the opportunity. Don't let me be overcome by the normality of the people around me. Keep me humble and protect me from guilt at the same time. Be with the family of seven that I was unable to place in*

a home before leaving.

Like I have prayed before—Be God in this situation!
Amen

And God can use you. That is the truth, even if you don't believe it today.

As you submit your life to Him and seek His will and direction for your life, keep a few notes on His activity in your life. Keep track of the needs He brings to your attention. Pray about them and how you can be involved. And keep track of His answered prayers. Our hope is you'll go far beyond five pages.

That's our purpose. To get you involved. Fearlessly. Faithfully. Hopefully. It's less about what you personally have to offer God and man than it is about your willingness to be used by God to serve man.

Once, a discouraged young man spoke to an older, stronger Christian brother. He challenged his believing brother for answers. The answers came when the older man tried to open the large, double-sized drawer at the bottom of his antique wooden desk.

At first, the drawer wouldn't open. Papers jammed it shut. So, the gentleman guided his hand inside and held down the sprawling sheets while patiently and slowly rocking the clogged drawer open. Inside were hundreds of pages of accounts of answered prayers and "God sightings" — times when God made Himself clearly and unmistakably True. It didn't take long for the younger man to repent — to change his mind — and to heed the testimony of an elder who had seen Jesus many times, and had taken notes.

You can be a faithful encourager. Even if you have little "faith-courage" today. Start your faith and service journey by writing in this five-page journal. It's a beginning. Maybe a new beginning for you. But the Lord can bless it and bear fruit from it — even a thousand-fold.

Go for it.

JOURNAL— DAY 1

JOURNAL— DAY 2

JOURNAL— DAY 3

JOURNAL— DAY 4

JOURNAL— DAY 5

KATRINA Soul Search

ADDITIONAL RESOURCES

The Art Of Listening Prayer
Finding God's Voice Amidst Life's Noise
by Seth Barnes

This interactive devotional is for the person who isn't satisfied with a dry faith. If you're dying to hear God's voice, the good news is that you can! Jesus is the door, and He has opened Himself up to you. He wants to put the "personal" back in the personal relationship that we tell others we have.

A personal relationship with God. What does it really mean? If God loves His people, couldn't it be that He desires to speak one-on-one with us? If so, wouldn't our first priority be to learn how to hear from Him?

Explore what it means to experience prayer that really is two-way. Using the Bible as a foundation, you can go way beyond theory and grow in the practice of listening prayer. This devotional will help you do it.

A Warrior's Journal
Winning The Sacred Struggle
By Seth Barnes

Early church history shows us that in a little more than 300 years, Christianity went from a small band of desperate men to the official religion of the Roman world. How did this happen?

It happened because of the absolute conviction of Jesus' disciples. They were warriors for the faith!

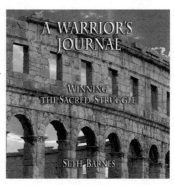

"A Warrior's Journal" is a long overdue resource organized to help you not just learn, but to practice the foundations of life as a warrior. This 9 week, 252 page companion, will turn your prayer life into a conversation, your Christianity into a passion, and the victory of battle into a lifestyle.

**To Order These Books and
Additional Copies of *Katrina Soul Search* go to
www.PraxisPublishing.com**

NOTES

KATRINA Soul Search